DINOSAURS
AND PREHISTORIC CREATURES

FEATURING NORTH AMERICAN DINOSAURS

MODERN PUBLISHING
A DIVISION OF UNISYSTEMS, INC.
NEW YORK, NEW YORK 10022

PRINTED IN ITALY
SERIES UPC#11985

Introduction

Millions of years ago, dinosaurs roamed the earth. But it is only within the last hundred years that humankind has known of the existence of these strange, diverse, and wondrous creatures. Their fossilized bones and teeth, discovered in the earth, are the clues that have led scientists on an investigative journey, unraveling the mystery, piecing together the long-buried facts about these creatures: their appearance, their habits, their development and sudden extinction.

From the enormous Sauropods, like the Apatosaurus, huge but peaceful creatures weighing many tons, to the unusual Ceratopsians, like the Triceratops, heavily-armored living "tanks" with horns that projected from their heads; from the eerie Pterosaurs, winged reptiles who soared on the wind currents, to the mighty Carnosaurs, like Tyrannosaurus Rex, king of the earth for its time here; the variety and complexity of the types of dinosaurs has fascinated us since humans first learned of the existence of Earth's first "tenants."

This book, and its companion volume, *Dinosaurs of the Land, Sea and Air,* present these creatures in an entertaining style. Stories give the reader a glimpse into each dinosaur's typical day. Exciting illustrations draw us further into this colorful world.

In addition, a "Facts about Dinosaurs" chapter is provided for those readers interested in learning more about these strange and fascinating creatures. An extensive glossary is included for quick, easy reference about the dinosaurs that appear in this book.

Take a journey back in time to the age of the amazing, incredible dinosaurs.

Table of Contents

Rhamphorhynchus

Pteranodon

Pterodactyl

Ankylosaurus

Dimetrodon

Iguanodon

Tricondon

Chapter One
Ankylosaurus

Written by Rupert Oliver
Illustrated by Bernard Long

Archaeopteryx

Ichthyosaurus

Plesiosaurus

Deinonychus

Nothosaurus

The sun was spreading its strong rays across the land. The mist of early morning had gone and a Stenonychosaurus had just returned from the hunt to rest. Its large eyes meant that it could hunt well in the dim light, catching animals that were still half asleep. However, the bright light of day hurt its eyes and Stenonychosaurus ran into the bushes after a hard night's work.

The Stenonychosaurus had caught a small, furry mammal to eat. As it trotted toward the undergrowth with its prey, the Stenonychosaurus disturbed another dinosaur, the Ankylosaurus, who was bedded down nearby.

Ankylosaurus raised herself to her feet and smelled the air. It smelled clean and fresh. The weather had been growing warmer over the past few days. The insects buzzed in and out of the flowers. Soon it would be summer.

Ankylosaurus was hungry. She had to spend nearly all the day eating to satisfy her hunger. There were new shoots and young plants in the hills now. The warmer days had brought them out. Ankylosaurus liked to eat the new shoots. They were juicy and tender. Some of the older leaves were too tough to chew and during the winter Ankylosaurus found very little food. Now that the warm weather had come, there would be plenty of food.

Slowly, Ankylosaurus walked off in search of food. She soon came to a large bush covered in beautiful, sweet-smelling flowers. Ankylosaurus was not interested in the flowers. She wanted to eat the tasty new leaves around the flowers.

As Ankylosaurus was happily munching away a Gravitholus ran past. Ankylosaurus did not often see bonehead dinosaurs such as this on their own. Perhaps the Gravitholus had lost a courtship fight.

15

As the sun climbed into the sky and the day became hotter, Ankylosaurus continued to eat. She chewed away happily on the young leaves of the bush. When she had finished these she moved on to the next bush. After a while, Ankylosaurus had eaten all the young shoots on the clump of bushes and she moved to look for more food.

Her search took her to the edge of one of the steep slopes that fell away to the lowlands. Below her, Ankylosaurus could see the thick vegetation that covered the land. A heat haze shimmered over the hot jungle. She saw another clump of bushes and turned to walk towards them.

As Ankylosaurus turned, a mighty roar filled the air and the ground rocked beneath her feet. In panic she looked around to see what could have caused such a frightening noise. Then it sounded even louder and the ground shook more violently. Ankylosaurus felt herself falling as the hillside collapsed beneath her. Her powerful legs could not hold on as she slipped down the steep slope.

No matter how Ankylosaurus struggled to find a foothold she just kept on slipping. She slipped and slid for a long time. When Ankylosaurus finally stopped, she was at the foot of a long, steep slope of gravel and loose soil. It was down this slope she had fallen.

Ankylosaurus was a little dazed, but she was not badly hurt. Her sudden arrival had startled a Dromiceiomimus. The frightened dinosaur ran off into the bushes.

Ankylosaurus looked about her. Apart from the slope, she was surrounded by dense bushes and the air was hot and humid. There was no way she could climb back up the slope so Ankylosaurus pushed through the undergrowth.

Ankylosaurus had no trouble forcing a way through the jungle. She was big and strong, and could push aside most of the plants. Ankylosaurus tried to eat some of the plants, but they were hard and tough. She began to long for the soft shoots of the hill plants.

Suddenly the jungle ended. Ankylosaurus stood on a slight rise overlooking a river. Along the sandy banks of the river were groups of Parasaurolophus. Many of the duckbill dinosaurs were crouched over mud nests that contained eggs. As soon as they saw Ankylosaurus, a pair of large Parasaurolophus ran toward her, uttering fierce noises. Ankylosaurus was puzzled. Usually duckbills were quiet and inoffensive. Now it looked as if they would attack her. She decided to retreat into the jungle.

As Ankylosaurus pushed her way through the undergrowth she realized it was getting less dense. Ankylosaurus also noticed that one of the plants had some tender new leaves on it. She stopped to eat.

There came a loud rustling noise from the depths of the jungle. A large animal was approaching Ankylosaurus. Ankylosaurus looked around to see what was coming and froze in sudden terror. The new charging animal was a ferocious Tyrannosaurus Rex. As Ankylosaurus watched in alarm another Tyrannosaurus appeared.

There was only one way that Ankylosaurus would be safe from attack. She lay flat on the ground and swung her clubbed tail around. The Tyrannosaurus clawed savagely at Ankylosaurus but her armor protected her. The tough bony shell was strong enough to stop even the most powerful kick from the hungry meat eater. For several terrifying minutes the powerful killer dinosaur clawed and bit at Ankylosaurus. At last Ankylosaurus managed to hit one of the Tyrannosaurs with her tail. The meat-eater let out a bellow of pain and rage. Then it moved away from Ankylosaurus.

Suddenly another dinosaur appeared out of
the forest. The Alamosaurus had been feeding on the
tree tops but turned in alarm when she heard the
Tyrannosaurs. The Tyrannosaurs saw the
Alamosaurus. It would make a much easier meal
than Ankylosaurus, so they started to chase the
Alamosaurus.

Ankylosaurus remained flat on the ground. She was afraid the meat eaters would return. After a while Ankylosaurus stood up. She could not see the Tyrannosaurs. Perhaps they had caught the Alamosaurus and were busy eating. Ankylosaurus had been very frightened by the attack.

Ankylosaurus then decided to move on. The plants were more like those that she enjoyed eating. It seemed as if the ground was rising. Ankylosaurus was nearing her home in the hills. Then she heard the footsteps of a large animal behind her. She was alarmed in case it was another Tyrannosaur.

The newcomer was a Triceratops. The great horned dinosaur was a plant eater and would not attack Ankylosaurus. As she watched, the Triceratops started roaring and stamping the ground. Something was wrong.

Another Triceratops appeared. The two horned dinosaurs turned to face each other. Then they charged. The ground vibrated as the two heavy beasts approached each other. With a tremendous crash the dinosaurs met head on. They backed away from each other and charged again. The Triceratops were engaged in a courtship fight. Ankylosaurus watched them for a while, and then moved on in search of more juicy young shoots and leaves.

Ever since Ankylosaurus had left the river she had been traveling toward the hills. Now she found herself back among the bushes that she liked to eat.

As Ankylosaurus chewed hungrily on the tender shoots of the hill plants, the leaves suddenly parted. A small Parksosaurus shot out from cover. Hot on its heels came a Saurornitholestes. The chase continued until the Saurornitholestes leaped on the Parksosaurus and killed it. The vicious claw on the hind foot of Saurornitholestes brought down the other dinosaur with one blow.

Ankylosaurus took no notice of the chase. She was happy to be back among plants she could eat and where there was no sign of Tyrannosaurs. As the sun began to sink behind the horizon Ankylosaurus lay down and closed her eyes. It had been an eventful day and Ankylosaurus was very tired.

Dimorphodon

Brachiosaurus

Dilophosaurus

Lystrosaurus

Rutiodon

Chapter Two

Brachiosaurus

Written by Rupert Oliver
Illustrated by Roger Payne

Mamenchisaurus

Plateosaurus

Chasmosaurus

Protoceratops

The air was hot and humid. The sun beat down from a clear sky onto the parched earth. A small Coelurus stirred in the bushes, then dashed forward hungrily. It soon ran out of energy and the Laopteryx it was chasing easily escaped into the trees. It was so hot that the Coelurus could not be bothered to hunt aggressively. The slightest effort made the animal even hotter. Coelurus looked around as a butterfly fluttered past and then settled down to rest.

High above Coelurus the swaying neck of Brachiosaurus reached high into the trees. She was looking for food among the high branches where other animals had eaten before her. The branches were stripped of all leaves.

Brachiosaurus was feeling the heat as well. The glaring sun beat down upon her back and her neck, making her feel uncomfortable. A slight breeze stirred the branches and Brachiosaurus caught a familiar and welcome scent of water. Wherever there was water, Brachiosaurus knew, it would be cooler. She set off in the direction of the water.

After pushing through the trees for a while, Brachiosaurus emerged onto the banks of a wide river. In the river, a young Camptosaurus and a Haplocanthosaurus wallowed in the mud. Brachiosaurus moved forward to join them. The mud looked cool and inviting.

Brachiosaurus rolled in the mud. It was beautifully cool compared with the hot, muggy air. Haplocanthosaurus must have felt cool enough, for it climbed out of the water and moved toward the trees. Then, the trees burst apart and a pair of Ceratosaurs leaped from the forest. The Haplocanthosaurus stopped in alarm. Ceratosaurs were fierce hunters and Haplocanthosaurus knew that danger was threatening. The plant eater turned to run, but the Ceratosaurs were too fast. Within seconds they had caught up with the dinosaur and were tearing into its soft flesh with their ferocious teeth and claws. It was not long before Haplocanthosaurus sank to the ground and the Ceratosaurs began their meal.

Brachiosaurus was worried. Ceratosaurs were as dangerous to her as to the unfortunate Haplocanthosaurus. She began to move off in the opposite direction. When a pack of Allosaurs suddenly appeared, she was frightened. Allosaurs were even bigger and fiercer than Ceratosaurs. Luckily, the Allosaurs were not interested in hunting, they had smelled the blood from Haplocanthosaurus. As Brachiosaurus backed away in alarm, the Allosaurs rushed toward the Ceratosaurs.

The Allosaurs began roaring loudly and displaying their teeth and claws. The Ceratosaurs were also displaying, but they were much smaller and not as powerful. As Brachiosaurus watched, one of the Allosaurs dashed forward and the Ceratosaurs ran away into the forest. The Allosaurs settled down to a stolen meal.

Brachiosaurus moved away from the river and away from the terrible hunters. It was still very hot and sultry, but a few clouds were beginning to appear in the sky. As Brachiosaurus pushed through the tall trees she disturbed a Dryosaurus and a Nanosaurus which had been chewing on some bushes. They scampered off for a short distance and then stopped. The air was so oppressive that the slightest movement was too much effort.

A distant roll of thunder reverberated through the air. Brachiosaurus stopped and looked around her. She shook her head in the still air. Then, the thunder boomed out again.

Quite suddenly the sky grew black as huge, dark clouds covered the sun. Lightning flashed across the sky, leaping from cloud to cloud and it became almost as dark as twilight.

Then, it began to rain in torrents. The rain was so heavy that Brachiosaurus could hardly see any distance at all and the forest around her dissolved into indistinct shapes hidden by the driving sheets of rain. Brachiosaurus felt the air cooling as the rain fell and the lightning flashed. It was a great relief after the oppressive heat, to feel cool water running down her neck and off her flanks.

Then, the rain stopped. Brachiosaurus looked around in surprise. In place of the gushing waters and dark skies of a moment earlier, there was bright sunshine. The ground underfoot was very wet and slippery and great pools of water lay all around. From the hillside a torrent of water ran down the slope toward the level ground. There had been so much rain that it could not soak into the ground and it was running off to find an outlet. The running water spread out when it reached the valley and Brachiosaurus could see that it had brought the body of an Othnielia with it. Perhaps the small dinosaur had been drowned in the sudden flood.

Brachiosaurus was moving off when a deep rumble made her turn in alarm. She had never heard such a sound before. It was not thunder. It sounded like no animal she had ever encountered. Then, as Brachiosaurus watched, the whole hillside seemed to twist and writhe. The rumbling grew louder as the soil, trees and plants on the hill crashed down into the valley. The heavy rain must have waterlogged the soil and undermined its hold on the hill. When the rumbling had stopped a jumble of fallen trees and mud spread around the foot of the hill.

Brachiosaurus realized just how hungry she was and looked around for some food. At a clump of trees not very far away, a Diplodocus was browsing on some of the lower branches. Perhaps there would be some good food there. Brachiosaurus moved toward the trees, passing a Stegosaurus on her way. The trees were full of tasty leaves and Brachiosaurus munched contentedly in the cool air which had followed the storm. It was no longer so hot and oppressive and Brachiosaurus felt much better.

Dimorphodon

Brachiosaurus

Dilophosaurus

Lystrosaurus

Rutiodon

Chapter Three

Dilophosaurus

Written by Rupert Oliver
Illustrated by Andrew Howatt

Mamenchisaurus

Plateosaurus

Chasmosaurus

Protoceratops

Segisaurus pushed through the undergrowth.
Somewhere she had heard a small animal
moving. Taking care not to make too much noise,
Segisaurus crept around a bush and saw her prey.
A tiny furry mammal was chewing away at a large
millipede. So intent was the mammal that it did not
notice Segisaurus.

Segisaurus dashed forward, arms
outstretched and jaws gaping. Then, the mammal
saw Segisaurus, but it was too late. The dinosaur
grabbed the small creature and plunged her teeth
deep into the warm flesh. As soon as Segisaurus
started her meal she was disturbed by a tremendous
noise. A massive foot came down and struck the
ground right next to Segisaurus.

The great foot belonged to Dilophosaurus. Dilophosaurus was hungry. He had not eaten anything for several days. Luckily for Segisaurus, Dilophosaurus was not interested in small animals. He needed prey more suited to his size. Segisaurus scampered off into the undergrowth. At that moment the earth moved beneath Dilophosaurus' feet. For a few seconds the ground swayed and Dilophosaurus almost lost his balance. Then, everything was still. Dilophosaurus was puzzled.

Dilophosaurus was now very hungry and as the ground was no longer swaying, he moved down to the beach to see if there was anything to eat. When he emerged onto the seashore he saw something which interested him.

Not far away was a Plesiosaur which had come ashore to lay her eggs. Dilophosaurus knew that Plesiosaurs could only move slowly and that they tasted delicious. Dilophosaurus chased after the Plesiosaur. In fear, Plesiosaur dragged herself along on her flippers in the hope of reaching the ocean. Just as she got to the surf, Dilophosaurus caught up with her. As the surf splashed around them, the two reptiles grappled with each other. Dilophosaurus tried to get his teeth around the vulnerable neck of Plesiosaur while the sea reptile attempted desperately to get away into deeper water where she would be safe.

After a while Dilophosaurus was successful in sinking his teeth into the neck of the Plesiosaur and the surf became stained red with the blood of the dying reptile.

Dilophosaurus dragged his kill up the beach, away from the waves. Once again the ground suddenly shook. Dilophosaurus looked around in alarm, but he could not see anything of which to be frightened. He did not notice the smoke coming from an island out to sea.

A loud roar startled Dilophosaurus. Emerging from the trees was another Dilophosaurus. He smelled the fresh meat of the Plesiosaur and he was very hungry. The new arrival advanced on Dilophosaurus roaring loudly and displaying his crests in an attempt to frighten Dilophosaurus. Dilophosaurus stood his ground and shook his crests at the other dinosaur. Then, a female Dilophosaurus appeared from the trees and joined her mate in frightening Dilophosaurus. Dilophosaurus realized he was no match for two dinosaurs so he took a last bite of meat and backed away.

Dilophosaurus was very disappointed. He had lost his kill and was still very hungry. Now, he would have to find some other food. There was no other creature along the beach, for the roaring of the dinosaurs had frightened everything away.

Dilophosaurus climbed up the steep hill behind the beach to look for food farther inland. Then, the earth shuddered one more time. This was immediately followed by a tremendous explosion and the island off the coast disappeared in a sheet of flame. A cloud of smoke shot up from the island high into the air.

The Dilophosaurs on the beach looked up from their meal as the explosions continued and all the animals fell silent as the island continued to rip itself apart.

Dilophosaurus gazed out at the island in surprise and fright. As he watched, the ball of smoke grew thicker and larger. The sea around the island was tossed violently about while the explosions continued with devastating effect. Before long, the great cloud of smoke and ash had risen until it blotted out the sun. It was almost as dark as a thunderstorm.

Then, a sudden whooshing noise startled Dilophosaurus from his gazing. He looked around and saw a huge boulder fall from the sky. Again, the noise like a tremendous wind came and another rock smashed into the ground. Dilophosaurus was very confused. Nothing like this had ever happened before and he was frightened.

Rocks were falling all around him now. Dilophosaurus moved toward the trees, perhaps they would give him some shelter from the falling rocks. Then, one of the rocks plummeted down and crashed into Dilophosaurus. Dilophosaurus gave a roar of pain and fell to the ground. His leg was hurting and he could not get up.

As Dilophosaurus lay on the ground nursing his wound, a new and strange sound came to his ears. It was like the booming of distant thunder and it was coming from out of the sea. Dilophosaurus looked down to the beach. The other two Dilophosaurs were still eating the Plesiosaur, but something had changed. The water was running out to sea, leaving a broad stretch of sand.

The booming grew louder and Dilophosaurus looked in alarm as a wall of water, many feet high rushed shoreward from the ocean. The enormous wave swept aside the two Dilophosaurs on the beach and they disappeared beneath the water. Then, it smashed into the hill where Dilophosaurus was resting. Water splashed everywhere and even Dilophosaurus was drenched.

When the massive wave had subsided the beach was left empty. There were no Dilophosaurs and no Plesiosaur. The island continued to belch smoke, but the explosions had stopped.

Dilophosaurus tried to stand up. His leg was very painful where it had been hit by the rock. Eventually, he got to his feet and hobbled off to look for food. Dilophosaurus had been hurt, but he would soon be better.

Rhamphorhynchus

Pteranodon

Pterodactyl

Ankylosaurus

Dimetrodon

Iguanodon

Tricondon

70

Chapter Four

Dimetrodon

Written by Rupert Oliver
Illustrated by Bernard Long

Archaeopteryx

Ichthyosaurus

Plesiosaurus

Deinonychus

Nothosaurus

A Petrolacosaurus hurried out onto a fallen log to warm himself in the sun. Through the leaves overhead, the early morning sun was shining. Petrolacosaurus had come to lie in the sun because it gave him energy.

Suddenly, Petrolacosaurus saw something move a short distance away. A leathery, sail-like fin came in sight. The fin belonged to one of the largest and most dangerous hunters, the Dimetrodon. At once Petrolacosaurus dashed back into the dense undergrowth.

Dimetrodon moved so that the warming rays of the sun shone on his sail. It was good to feel the sun warming his body. Soon he would be warm enough to go in search of food. Dimetrodon was hungry and he wanted meat.

As the sun rose in the sky, its heat warmed
Dimetrodon until he felt able to start hunting.
Dimetrodon raised himself up on his powerful legs
and walked off through the forest. As he walked, his
feet slipped in the sticky mixture of mud and fallen
leaves. It was always damp near the great delta as it
often rained.

As Dimetrodon pushed his way through the plants he kept a careful watch for any signs of life. He saw a small Cacops come out of the undergrowth. Even a small animal like this would make a tasty meal for Dimetrodon. Dimetrodon did not attack it. He had attacked a Cacops before. That was when Dimetrodon had broken one of his teeth on the bony plates on Cacops' back. He did not want to break another tooth, so he let the Cacops go. Unseen by either of the two animals, a tiny Cardiocephalus watched from a muddy pool.

A loud scream echoed through the lush plants. An animal was in trouble. When an animal is hurt, it is easier to catch. Perhaps this meant an easy meal for Dimetrodon. With a burst of speed, Dimetrodon plodded toward the sound.

Edaphosaurus was usually far too big for Dimetrodon to catch. However, when it became exhausted in the mud, Edaphosaurus would make an easy meal. Dimetrodon decided to wait. All the time the sun was getting hotter. Insects appeared and soon the air was alive with buzzing flies, bugs and dragonflies.

The Edaphosaurus continued to struggle in the mud. Suddenly it pulled itself free and Dimetrodon changed his mind about attacking. Wading off through the shallows, Edaphosaurus continued the search for tasty shellfish. An Ophiderpeton slid out of the mud. It hurried away from the hungry Edaphosaurus, across the surface of the mud, before tunneling down again in search of water bugs.

Dimetrodon splashed along the edge of the smelly pond. The sun was high in the sky now. As Dimetrodon plodded along he noticed a new smell. It was the scent of fresh, clean water. Dimetrodon was thirsty. The new scent made him want to quench his thirst even more. Dimetrodon ran through the trees as fast as his legs would carry him.

Soon Dimetrodon was out of the forest. Ahead were the shores of a wide lake. The sudden appearance of the fierce meat eater frightened the lakeside creatures. They ran for cover. A pair of Cacops dashed along the shore. A Seymouria hurried into the shrubs to hide. Much larger animals, like Eryops, waddled off toward the water where they felt safer. Soon all was quiet and Dimetrodon walked down to the water's edge and drank the cool, clean refreshing water.

When Dimetrodon finished drinking, he looked around. The heads of the few Eryops broke the surface of the lake. Otherwise the only moving life was the insects flying through the air.

The sun was now very hot. It was so hot that Dimetrodon began to feel uncomfortable and tired. He knew that he would have to find a shady place to rest until the air became cooler. Dimetrodon walked back to the edge of the forest and settled down under a clump of tree ferns.

Dimetrodon dozed through the heat of the day, while the insects whirred back and forth and Eryops splashed in the lake searching for fish.

When the temperature began to drop, Dimetrodon stretched his legs. It would soon be cool enough for him to move about again. Just then a cool breeze blew off the lake. Dimetrodon moved around so that his sail-like fin would catch the breeze and cool him more quickly.

Suddenly, Dimetrodon heard loud footsteps behind him. There was something large moving just out of sight in the undergrowth. Dimetrodon poked his head through the leaves and saw the familiar sight of a Diadectes. Diadectes looked hot and tired. It would not be able to run very fast.

With a hungry roar Dimetrodon ran through
the undergrowth after the reptile. It saw Dimetrodon
and began to run as fast as it could. The ground
shook as the two reptiles lumbered along over the
slippery, mud-covered leaves. Then, ahead of
Diadectes, there was a shallow muddy pool.

In his panic, the heavy reptile jumped into the pool, spraying mud and water everywhere. An animal, which had been feeding in the pool, scrambled out of the way as Dimetrodon charged in after the Diadectes.

The Diadectes tried to struggle through the mud to the far side of the pool but his legs became stuck in the mud and he did not have enough strength to pull them free. Swiftly the deadly jaws of Dimetrodon closed round the throat of Diadectes and the reptile breathed no more.

Without moving from the pond, Dimetrodon tore at the carcass of Diadectes. With his strong teeth, Dimetrodon tore great chunks of meat from the body. He gulped them down without even chewing.

It was a long time before Dimetrodon had satisfied his hunger. Finally, Dimetrodon crawled to the edge of the pool and lay down to rest. The air was growing chilly as the sun went down. Dimetrodon found a place to lie down for the night. He would not need to hunt again for several days.

Diplodocus

Pteranodon

Woolly Mammoth

Chapter Five
Diplodocus

Written by Ron Wilson
Illustrated by Doreen Edwards

Allosaurus

Hypsilophodon

Ichthyosaurus

The herd of Diplodocus had grown large. There had always been enough food for all. Each year the youngsters had stayed with the herd. Now things were different. Food had become scarce. Neither old nor young Diplodocus had enough to eat.

Some older members of the herd guarded the little food which was left. They rationed it out carefully. The creatures were allowed to feed early before the sun came up. Then they sought the meager shelter of the bare stems of one of the old trees. The Diplodocus had other problems. They had to protect their food from other plant-eaters like Brontosaurus and Brachiosaurus.

Several older members of the herd were on duty guarding the plants when they were disturbed by a noise behind them. There were cracking branches and a general rumpus. The Diplodocus let out their customary warning call.

The advance continued. Large shapes appeared in
the undergrowth all around. Allosaurus had appeared
on all sides. The Diplodocus knew what this meant.
They let forth cries for help as the intruders moved
closer. The shrieks from the startled Diplodocus spread
far and wide. Some herd members were sleeping; others
resting. It was some time before the terrified cries
reached all the members.

The younger Diplodocus had never been
summoned like this before. As they saw other members
of the herd move they followed them. Soon dozens of
old and young were coming from all directions.
Unceasing cries for help still came thick and fast from
somewhere among the mass of dying vegetation.

The first arrivals saw strange and unfamiliar shapes in front of them. They stopped in their tracks. Most had never come across this situation before. They had watched single members of the herd being attacked. They had never seen so many large creatures. Panic cries came from the Diplodocus guarding the food supply. As other Diplodocus arrived at the scene of activity they too slowly came to a halt. The Allosaurus remained immobile too. The herd of Diplodocus was not sure what the next move was.

The cries ceased. Diplodocus and their enemies faced each other. The silence was intense. The quiet was broken somewhere in the distance as a Brachiosaurus called loudly to its mates.

Then, without any kind of signal the Allosaurus advanced. They charged toward the Diplodocus guarding the trees. For a moment there was utter confusion. The old Diplodocus stood their ground, letting out cries of anguish. The rest of the herd seemed uncertain. Some stayed where they were; others backed away.

The cries turned to terror as the Allosaurus attacked. Sharp teeth and claws sank into the Diplodocus' leathery skin. There was no hope. The old Diplodocus were no match for their attackers.

Each of the onlookers realized this. A few stayed
to watch. Most fled away into the withered vegetation,
their long necks poking out from the horsetails and
ferns.

The herd split up. Some groups went one way;
some another. Each continued on their slow lumbering
way with hardly a backward glance. Normally the
Diplodocus didn't have to move far. Today was
different. If they were going to survive they would have
to go a long way away. Instinct told them that once the
Allosaurus had finished off the old Diplodocus they
would look for other members of the herd.

They plodded clumsily on their way. In their haste they scattered numbers of small mammals feeding on the ground. A group of younger Diplodocus stayed together. A young female stopped for breath. She had never been so far in her life. She called out. It was a call for help. Most of them didn't seem to hear her call and continued on their way.

However, one young male Diplodocus did stop. He turned around to gaze at the frightened creature. He moved toward her, glad to help one of his kind.

They communicated, and the young male Diplodocus was soon aware of the female's problems. As they rested the young dinosaur was ever on the alert for danger.

After a while they moved forward slowly. Both were hungry. The Diplodocus searched until they found a few shrivelled leaves. They shared them. The older of the two made sure that the younger one had food to eat.

The male Diplodocus didn't recognize the area. There were no landmarks that he knew. The juvenile Diplodocus sensed a note of alarm in the older male's manner. She wasn't sure what it meant.

The two dinosaurs trudged slowly onward. The
male paused now and then to try and get a bearing. He
made continuous calls, listening anxiously for a reply.
There was none. He had never been on his own
before, and fear overcame him.

In unfamiliar territory he was ever on the
lookout for enemies. The earlier events were still vivid in
his memory.

With the sun high overhead it was very hot. The male Diplodocus signalled to his female companion that they must soon try and find shelter. They were hungry and thirsty, conscious of the hot sun beating down on their leathery skins.

Suddenly a short distance in front of them, the older Diplodocus saw a rock. He approached it with caution. A small lizard scampered away into the undergrowth and startled him.

He indicated to the female Diplodocus to stay where she was. He thoroughly surveyed the rock, but there was no sign of life. He turned to the female Diplodocus, urging her to come toward the overhanging ledge. With room for both to shelter they stood very still, glad of time to rest.

Eventually the temperature dropped, and the two hungry creatures moved off. The male Diplodocus led the way. They searched every bush for food. They found a leaf here and there and even nibbled at the rough branches.

The older Diplodocus sniffed the air. Suddenly, he caught the smell of conifers which drifted toward his nostrils. He headed eagerly in the direction of the scent, moving more quickly than he had done since escaping from the Allosaurus. The female stayed close behind. The male's pace quickened, the female finding it difficult to keep up.

In front of them a whole plantation of lush vegetation came into view. Both creatures ate more than their fill and then wandered lazily to a nearby rock to rest.

The male dinosaur was awakened by faint sounds. He recognized them. They were from his own kind. He woke his younger companion.

Both creatures called back in unison. Soon the area was echoing with the sounds of many Diplodocus. After wandering far and wide they had all arrived in the same place.

There was plenty of food for all in the area which the young dinosaurs had found first.

Rhamphorhynchus

Pteranodon

Pterodactyl

Ankylosaurus

Dimetrodon

Iguanodon

Tricondon

Chapter Six
Plesiosaurus

Written by Rupert Oliver
Illustrated by Andrew Howatt

Archaeopteryx

Ichthyosaurus

Plesiosaurus

Deinonychus

Nothosaurus

The sun sparkled on the waves and the surf crashed on the beach. A cool breeze rippled the surface of the warm, sun-drenched sea. Suddenly a long neck rose up from the water. On top of the snake-like neck was a small head. Plesiosaurus had come to lay her eggs.

Plesiosaurus eyed the broad beach carefully. There was often danger on the beach. Plesiosaurus could only see a group of Cetiosaurus and Pelorosaurus on the beach. Such plant-eating dinosaurs were no danger to Plesiosaurus, so she began to lumber up onto the beach. Plesiosaurus used her strong flippers to drag herself over the sand. She was not very agile and was always clumsy on land.

Plesiosaurus lumbered over the warm sand. The sun quickly dried her skin. When Plesiosaurus was above the high-tide mark she began to dig. She knew that her eggs would be safest if she buried them in the sand. Hunting animals would be less likely to find them and the sand would help to keep them warm.

Plesiosaurus worked busily with her front flippers. Her flippers were really built for swimming not for digging. After a time she had dug a hole that was deep enough. Plesiosaurus turned around and began to lay her eggs. The sand near Plesiosaurus suddenly began to move. There was something under the sand trying to get out.

As Plesiosaurus watched a small head broke the surface of the sand. Then another head appeared. The heads were followed by tiny Plesiosaurus. They belonged to the eggs of another Plesiosaurus which had laid her eggs on the beach a few weeks earlier. Soon there were dozens of baby Plesiosaurus on the beach. They all began to crawl towards the ocean. Then from out of the sky, a Rhamphorhynchus swooped down. It grabbed a baby Plesiosaurus in its jaws and flew off.

Other Rhamphorhynchus arrived and began to eat the babies. From the forest a Teinurosaurus appeared and dashed across the beach. Soon it too, was gobbling up the babies. Eventually about half the babies reached the safety of the sea. When Plesiosaurus's eggs hatched her young would have to face the same dangerous journey to the sea.

Plesiosaurus finished laying her eggs. She used her hind flippers to cover the eggs with the warm sand. She had only just finished when a terrible roar boomed across the beach.

Looking round in alarm, Plesiosaurus saw a pair of Megalosaurs at the edge of the forest. The fierce meat-eaters had seen Plesiosaurus. They began to run towards her. Plesiosaurus knew what would happen if these dinosaurs caught her. Her life was in danger.

Plesiosaurus dragged herself across the beach as fast as she could. She knew that if she could reach the water she would be safe. All the time the ferocious hunters were catching up with Plesiosaurus. She was very frightened. The pounding feet of the bellowing Megalosaurs were close behind. At last Plesiosaurus reached the water. She swam off leaving the hunters on the shore.

Plesiosaurus was glad to be back in the water. This was where she felt at home. The waves lapped over her body as she paddled out to sea. With strong, even strokes Plesiosaurus moved across the water surface. Now that she had laid her eggs, Plesiosaurus realized that she was hungry.

With her head held high Plesiosaurus could see a large area of ocean. A sudden flash of silver caught Plesiosaurus's eye. There was a school of fish just beneath the surface. Plesiosaurus gently paddled towards the fish. When she was close enough Plesiosaurus darted her head forward. Her jaws plunged into the water and emerged with a fish. Plesiosaurus quickly gobbled down the fish. Then her head struck out again and she caught another fish.

Suddenly Plesiosaurus realized that there were some creatures beneath her that were not fish. They looked like fish, but they were far larger. Then two of the creatures burst out of the water. They were Ichthyosaurs.

Just beneath the surface of the sea the
Ichthyosaurs dashed to and fro snapping up the fish
as fast as they could. Before long the fish had
scattered in all directions. The Ichthyosaurus moved
on in search of more fish. Plesiosaurus was still
hungry. She also would have to find more food.

The waves on the ocean were becoming larger and the wind was getting stronger. After a while Plesiosaurus was having to paddle up and down the waves because they were so large. Plesiosaurus was still looking for food, but she could not find any more fish.

As Plesiosaurus looked around a gigantic head burst through the water. The great jaws were filled with teeth and were almost half the size of Plesiosaurus's entire body. Plesiosaurus was frightened and began to swim off as fast as she could. The great head disappeared back beneath the water. When it reappeared the jaws were firmly grasping several cuttlefish. The giant beast was a Pliosaur. Plesiosaurus knew that the newcomer was no real danger to her. All this time dark clouds had been gathering and the waves had been getting larger and stronger. A storm was brewing.

In a very short time dark clouds had covered the entire sky and the wind had become a screaming gale. The waves towered over Plesiosaurus as she struggled to stay upright. One particular wave came crashing down on top of Plesiosaurus. The great weight of water entirely covered Plesiosaurus. Under the water Plesiosaurus could not breathe and she tried desperately to reach the surface again. Eventually she was able to take a breath of air.

High above Plesiosaurus, lightning flashed from cloud to cloud. Thunder rumbled out across the sky. Plesiosaurus was very frightened indeed. The gigantic waves continued to lash against her and the wind howled around her.

After many hours the wind became weaker. The huge, dark clouds drifted away and the sky was clear again. Soon the waves were smaller. The sea was almost calm. Plesiosaurus was able to swim without any difficulty. She sighted a school of fish and swam over to them. As her head dipped into the water to grab a fish, another animal flashed by. The fish were being hunted by a Metriorhynchus as well as by Plesiosaurus.

The Metriorhynchus took a few fish and then swam on. Plesiosaurus was left alone on the wide open sea. After a while she began eating fish again. She would have to build up her strength after fighting the terrible storm.

Dimorphodon

Brachiosaurus

Dilophosaurus

Lystrosaurus

Rutiodon

130

Chapter Seven

Protoceratops

Written by Rupert Oliver
Illustrated by Roger Payne

Mamenchisaurus

Plateosaurus

Chasmosaurus

Protoceratops

The long neck of Nemegtosaurus curved gracefully up to the branches. The small teeth took a small mouthful of leaves from the topmost branches which were swallowed instantly and another mouthful taken. The lower branches were being stripped of their greenery by a pair of Opisthocoelicaudia.

A quiet shuffling noise caused Nemegtosaurus to look down toward his feet. Brushing past him through the clearing was a small, four-legged dinosaur. The small Protoceratops was no threat to the giant Sauropods and they continued to eat.

Protoceratops pushed on through the forest. She was looking for a place to lay her eggs. The tough undergrowth of the forest was quite unsuitable for it would not shelter her eggs. Protoceratops was looking for some loose earth in which she could bury her eggs.

Nosing through the greenery of the palms, Protoceratops found herself by the banks of a river. The sloping banks were covered with sand and Protoceratops began to dig. When she had dug out a round hole, Protoceratops laid her eighteen eggs in three concentric circles. Then she brushed the sand back over the eggs. Having finished such hard work, Protoceratops was thirsty and she walked down to the river to drink.

No sooner had Protoceratops taken her first mouthful of water, than she heard a scrabbling noise behind her. Turning around she saw an Oviraptor digging up her eggs. Protoceratops knew that Oviraptor liked to eat eggs. She would have to protect her unhatched young somehow.

Lowering her head so as to present the hard bony frill to Oviraptor, Protoceratops charged forward. Oviraptor looked up. He fell back before the charging Protoceratops, then turned and ran away. Protoceratops was so angry that she did not stop when Oviraptor retreated. She continued to chase him blindly through the undergrowth, trampling plants beneath her thundering feet.

Suddenly Protoceratops emerged from the forest into the bright sunlight of a clearing. She stopped in fear. Right in front of her was a pack of Velociraptors. She knew how dangerous these dinosaurs could be, with the huge claws on their hind feet. Luckily the Velociraptors had not seen Protoceratops. They seemed to be watching something else. Quietly, Protoceratops backed into the foliage, hoping she would not be noticed.

The object of the Velociraptors' attention came into sight. It was a Homalocephale. As soon as the Homalocephale saw the Velociraptors it turned and fled. The pack of Velociraptors roared in excitement and plunged after their prey. As they disappeared from sight, Protoceratops moved back into the undergrowth.

As Protoceratops moved through the trees she
became aware of two large animals nearby. They
were eating the shoots and fruits of the bushes. The
large Nodosaurs turned and looked at Protoceratops
before continuing to feed.

Protoceratops suddenly realized just how hungry she was herself. She found a clump of low palms and began to slice off the spiky leaves with her sharp teeth. Whenever she bit through a stem the sweet, milky sap of the palm would ooze out. Protoceratops lapped the sap up hungrily, it was her favorite part of the plant.

After eating her fill of the palm plant and licking up the sap, Protoceratops was no longer hungry. It was then that she sensed something was wrong. She was not near her eggs and they might be in danger. Quickly she hurried through the trees to the river bank where she had laid her eggs. Thankfully nothing had happened to her nest. The sand was undisturbed and the eggs were safe. Protoceratops knew that until the eggs were hatched she would have to stay close to the river bank to protect the nest.

A large drop of water fell on Protoceratops' nose, causing her to shake her head. Then more drops fell all around and the trees began to sway as the wind became stronger. Protoceratops crouched under a bush as the rain fell more heavily and the wind grew stronger.

A bright flash of lightning streaked across the sky and a deep rumble of thunder boomed through the forest. Protoceratops huddled lower in fear. The rain was falling in torrents from the dark sky and the trees were twisting and lurching in the violent storm.

Heavy footsteps sounded from the trees and a huge Tarbosaurus ran from the forest toward the river. It had been frightened by the storm and was running in sheer panic. Just as the large dinosaur reached the river bank a bolt of lightning flashed down from the sky and struck the Tarbosaurus. The huge beast twisted in pain and then crashed to the ground. It lay still and did not move.

In time the storm passed and the sun came out. A Chingkankousaurus and a pair of Velociraptors came to scavenge food from the dead Tarbosaurus. Protoceratops did not dare move when such fierce meat eaters were nearby. She stayed huddled under the bushes. Evening was drawing on now and perhaps the hunters would leave when night came. Then Protoceratops could move out and eat some more palms and continue to keep an eye on her nest. One day soon her young would hatch.

Diplodocus

Pteranodon

Woolly Mammoth

Chapter Eight
Pteranodon

Written by Ron Wilson
Illustrated by Doreen Edwards

Allosaurus

Hypsilophodon

Ichthyosaurus

It was still dark when the old Pteranodon woke up. The younger Pterosaurs would have little to do with him. He was old and he didn't have as much energy as they did. He'd been out with them a few days earlier when they had stopped him from feeding at the old cove. They had made so much fuss that Pteranodon had gone off on his own. He had flown many miles and had found another bay.

It was a secret place and no Pterosaurs fed there. He had perched high above this new bay. Down below he could see the still clear waters spread out before him. Although it was deserted it was the sort of place that should have had plenty of fish. Pteranodon hadn't had time to search. Night was falling. He had to return to his roosting place.

So today was a special day. He was going to leave. If he didn't do it soon other Pterosaurs were bound to find the place. Of course his old body would soon be too fragile to carry him. It was the first chance he had had to set off on his own. He wanted to go to the new cove just for peace and quiet. It seemed an ideal place with enough food for the taking. Yet no other Pterosaurs fed there. He wondered why.

The cliffs were still very quiet. Around him the sky was a beautiful pink. The sun would soon be rising. All the other Pterosaurs were still asleep. There was no sound. This was just the time for Pteranodon to leave. Before he moved Pteranodon had to be sure that no other creature was awake. He moved carefully. He was not careful enough. He disturbed a piece of rock which went crashing to the beach below. It was so loud that it would be a miracle if the other Pterosaurs were not awakened.

Pteranodon watched and listened. Below him he saw the form of another Pteranodon. He knew that if he disturbed it it would warn all the other Pterosaurs. Then the whole cliff would be awake, and they would attack him.

He watched the creature carefully. It did not move. The sound had gone unnoticed by the sleeping animals. Pteranodon looked up above his head between the rocky cliffs. He could see the sky. He had enough room to launch himself without crashing into anything. He took off carefully from his resting place. His old limbs lifted him slowly above the cliffs. He managed to get away without making a sound.

He circled slowly before he headed south. The
old Pteranodon had flown the route to his feeding
ground many many times. He could probably have
gotten there blindfolded.

He flew slowly, his aging wings would not carry
him as fast as when he was younger. It was still early
and he must fly on before he took a rest. He got into
the strongest air currents.

He drifted inland not far from the coast. He was
sure there were a lot of enemies below. He had seen
many Tyrannosaurus on his other journeys. He flew
well above the tops of the trees. He was heading for his
usual feeding place. From high up he could see the long
shadows creeping over the countryside, as the sun came
up. He caught sight of many stirring dinosaurs below
him.

Borgen Edmonds

Once he made it to the old cove he would find it easier getting to the new bay. A short way in front of him was a well-known landmark. There was a small clump of trees which was used by some of the Pterosaurs as a resting place.

Pteranodon had travelled a long way. Every wing beat was more difficult. He felt very weary and he made his way to the group of trees. He flew around looking down to see whether any other creatures were there. He could not see any other signs of life. Pteranodon landed so that he could rest for a while. Soon something inside him told him he had to move. It wouldn't be long before the sun was fully up and every creature would be awake.

He felt better after a few minutes rest.
Pteranodon set off again, the air currents carrying him
much faster. Some distance in front was an outcrop of
rock. It roughly marked the halfway point of his flight
to his usual feeding place.

The old Pteranodon knew that there were very few resting places ahead, except for the jagged rock. He knew he must get there. Pteranodon passed over several clearings in the forest. He had time to look down. Already he could see signs of life. He saw an Euoplocephalus stirring. He heard a Tyrannosaurus bellowing. Soon the many sounds of the forest dwellers reached his ears. He was hungry so he had to keep going. He always knew he had to avoid danger.

Pteranodon would soon have to stop before the sun made it too hot for him to continue. If he didn't stop he would be seen. The rock was close. Pteranodon made for it. He circled it a few times before deciding it was safe to land. He grabbed it with his claws and soon settled down.

He had not eaten for a couple of days and he was very hungry. He had to stay here until tomorrow. Other Pterosaurs flew overhead. He looked up but he didn't recognize any from his particular flock.

Pteranodon looked down. He watched as a Triceratops fed on the fronds of one of the giant plants. The creature's body was large. It needed a great deal of food to satisfy its hunger. Soon it had stripped all the fronds from several plants.

In the distance another Triceratops fought savagely with one of its own kind. The old Pteranodon could hear the angry noises. He was very weary. The sounds became fainter. Soon he was asleep. He woke many hours later. The sun had set and everywhere was quiet and dark except for the light from a full moon.

Pteranodon knew he had to set off again. He
cleared the rock without a sound except for the flapping
of his leathery wings. Shortly he recognized the waters
of his usual feeding place below him. He needed to find
the new bay.

He soared higher, using the air currents. Soon he
had a much better view of the ground below him. He
circled for a few minutes and then went off in an
easterly direction. He flew on until he saw a glint of
silver below him. It was the moonlight shining on the
waters of the new bay.

Pteranodon flew high above the bay to see what it was like. He could not see clearly and he flew lower. There were many jagged rocks around the edge of the water. He had to fly carefully so that he didn't fly into them.

There was no sign of life. All the other creatures must be resting. Pteranodon landed on a rock overhanging the water. He settled down to wait for the coming day. Within a short time he was asleep.

When he awoke the sun was shining brightly. Pteranodon looked around him. He could not see anything. Nothing stirred on the rocks. Nothing moved in the grass. The waters of the bay were clear. Pteranodon could not see any fish. So this was why the other Pterosaurs had never been here to feed. There was nothing to eat. Pteranodon looked around him. He flew down for a closer look.

The Pterosaur had not eaten for two days now. He had flown a long way. He looked around for something to eat. He searched the bay but there was nothing. He needed food. The only place he knew was the old cove. He would have to go there and mix with the other Pterosaurs. He hoped they would not have noticed that he had been missing.

Pteranodon set off, the sun's position telling him which way to fly. The wide area of water of the old cove came into view. He could see the other Pterosaurs and he slowed down. He must fly in low so that he wouldn't be seen. Pteranodon did this and landed safely on a rocky ledge. He watched until the other Pterosaurs dived down to catch their food. Then he joined them. There was plenty of fish and he ate a lot. He kept his eye on the other Pterosaurs. They didn't seem to notice him.

He ate as much as he could and returned to a rock to digest. Soon it was time for the Pterosaurs to return to their nightly roosting sites. Pteranodon went with them. He flew a little way behind the rest of the group as he always did.

He arrived back a few minutes after the other Pterosaurs. He needed somewhere to rest. All the rocky ledges were full. He flew low over the tops of the cliffs. The other resting Pterosaurs attacked him. At last he found a vacant ledge some way from the other creatures. He landed gently and within minutes he had settled down and was asleep.

169

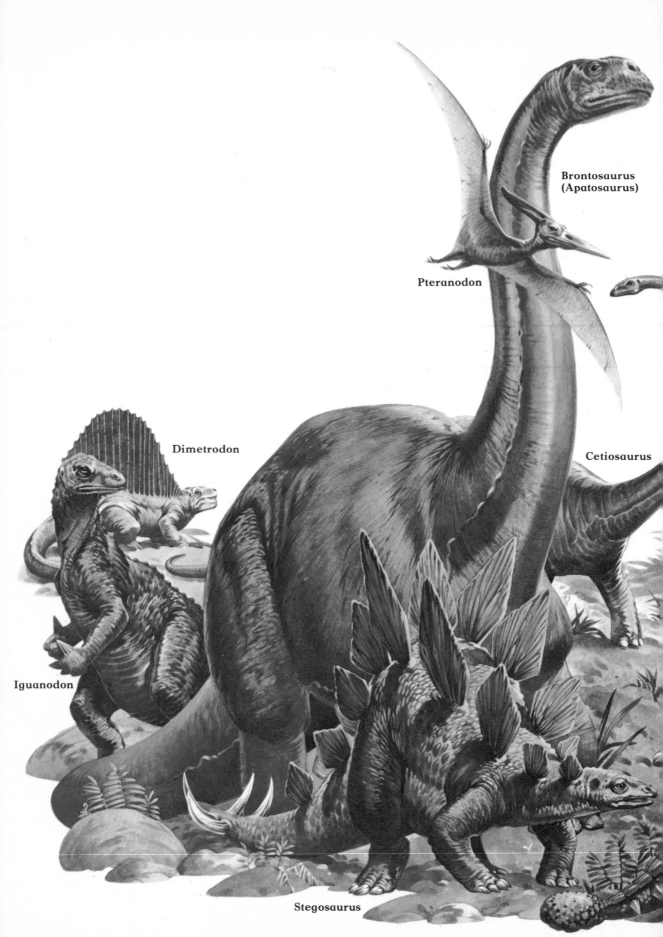

Brontosaurus
(Apatosaurus)

Pteranodon

Dimetrodon

Cetiosaurus

Iguanodon

Stegosaurus

170

Chapter Nine

Stegosaurus

Written by Angela Sheehan
Illustrated by John Francis

Tyrannosaurus

Triceratops

Parasaurolophus

Ornithomimus

Ankylosaurus

Despite his great size, Stegosaurus just could not get rid of the creature snapping round his feet. As fast as he turned, so the sharp-toothed little dinosaur ran round him, leaping and yapping at his sides. Stegosaurus was normally more than a match for Ornitholestes but he was now too tired to run or fight. The day had been long and hot, and he and his herd had walked a long way.

As the little dinosaur grew more excited, it began to take less and less care. At last it rushed towards Stegosaurus's back legs, and the great reptile took his chance. He swung his spiked tail and Ornitholestes fell to the ground, stunned and wounded. Stegosaurus plodded away.

The last glimmer of red was fading from the sky. Stegosaurus was so far behind his herd that he could hardly make out the animals' shapes against the trees ahead. By the time he reached the forest it was dark and he could see only shadows. But he could hear strange noises. He walked a little way, trying hard to stay awake. But he was too tired. Slowly his eyes closed and he sank into a deep sleep. All night the woods rang with howls, squawks and bellowing.

When Stegosaurus woke in the morning, the birds were already singing and the forest floor was speckled with light. He raised his head to look about, when suddenly the tree next to him shook and shuddered, and the bellowing noise he had heard at nightfall boomed out again. An Archaeopteryx squawked and flapped out of the swaying tree. Stegosaurus backed away as a huge gray shape loomed up before him.

Now he could see where the bellowing came from. The shape was a Brontosaurus. There was a whole herd of the giants marching through the swaying trees. Stegosaurus watched as they ripped the curving fronds from high on the trunks. He looked for his own herd but they were nowhere to be seen. So he followed the giants, staying just far enough behind not to disturb them.

Stegosaurus cropped the fronds on the forest floor, while the brontosaurs stretched their long necks to reach the topmost branches. After some time the herd stopped feeding and trundled out of the forest. Stegosaurus, close behind them, blinked in the bright sunshine and felt its warmth on his back. He marched quickly after the herd, away from the damp gloom of the woods.

Soon they reached a small waterhole. The brontosaurs waddled into the water, which was just deep enough to cover and cool their backs. Stegosaurus stayed on the bank and ate the thick ferns as the giants wallowed and bellowed. The ferns were hot and steaming in the fierce midday sun, and so high that Stegosaurus was completely hidden by them.

Suddenly he heard silence and then a rumble. Peering through the greenery, he saw the brontosaur herd clambering up the slippery bank of the pool. Only one animal could not keep up with the others as they galloped away. It was an old male. Behind him sped Megalosaurus, his great mouth gaping. The hungry reptile closed on the Brontosaurus and leaped on his back. But the old dinosaur's hide was too hard for Megalosaurus to grip and he lost his balance. As he fell, the Brontosaurus lashed out with his tail and left the attacker stunned.

Stegosaurus stayed well behind his screen of ferns until the dreadful creature had gone. Now all was quiet, but Stegosaurus was all alone. There were no other creatures to warn him of danger and none to hide or run with if danger came again. So he made his way back to the woods. It was cool beneath the trees, and there were many hiding places. He kept near to the edge of the wood, moving slowly and silently. The ground rose and the forest grew thicker.

All at once, Stegosaurus came to a break in the trees. He heard the sound of rushing water, and there in front of him was a waterfall. The water tumbled down a steep slope, splashed on the rocks below, and babbled noisily away. Stegosaurus drank from the cool stream and then followed its course.

After a time, the stream widened and the fish-filled water began to flow more gently. Stegosaurus rested for a while and then went on. He had not gone far when he heard a sound he knew well. It was the call of a female Stegosaurus ready to mate. He could not see her, so he headed for the clump of bushes from which the noise had come. As he neared them, he caught sight of the female and quickened his pace. But just as he reached her, another male Stegosaurus came roaring towards him.

The animal stopped a few paces away and growled fiercely. Stegosaurus saw that his rival was old: two of the spikes on his tail were broken, and his hide was pitted with the scars of old wounds. Stegosaurus wanted the female for himself. So he challenged the old male, by growling back at him and charging at him.

The old male charged too, but he was no
match for the younger Stegosaurus. After a short fight,
the old animal lumbered away, slowly but unhurt.
Stegosaurus approached the female.

He walked towards her, turning his head from side to side and swinging his tail. She growled a warning to keep away. But he took no notice. Instead he walked slowly round and round her, still swishing his tail. After a while, she stopped growling and let him come even closer. Then she allowed him to mate with her.

The two animals stayed by the river until the evening sun began to color the cliffs and the shadows of the cycads grew longer. Soon, the insects that had hovered and darted all day over the river were gone. It was almost night.

The female Stegosaurus listened to the sound of her herd calling as they lumbered off to rest. Then she and her new mate set off to join them. Stegosaurus would once again have other animals to travel with. And his mate would soon lay her eggs.

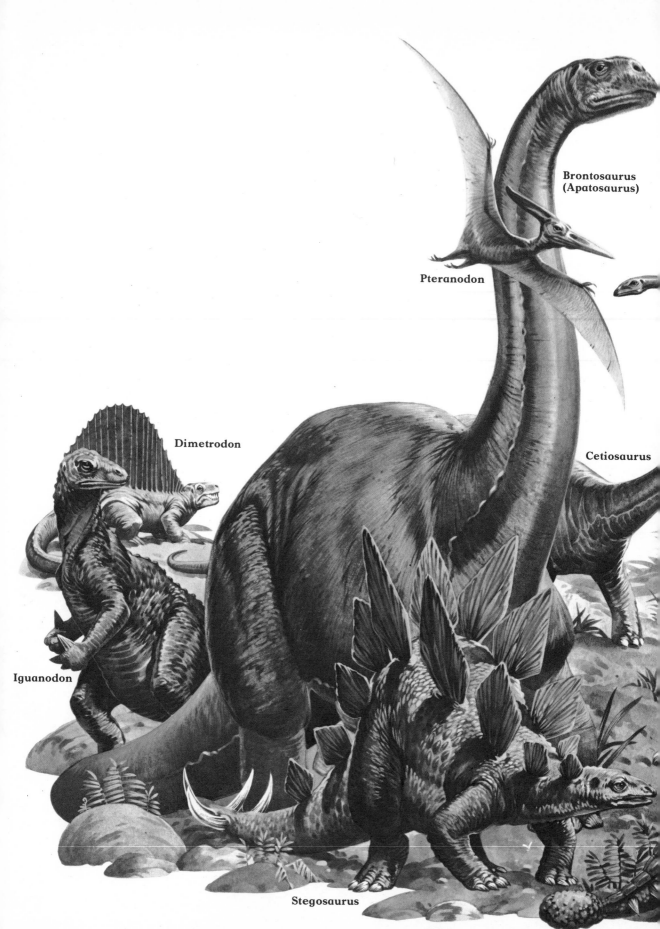

Brontosaurus
(Apatosaurus)

Pteranodon

Cetiosaurus

Dimetrodon

Iguanodon

Stegosaurus

190

Chapter Ten

Tyrannosaurus

Written by Angela Sheehan
Illustrated by George Thompson

Tyrannosaurus

Triceratops

Parasaurolophus

Ornithomimus

Ankylosaurus

Tyrannosaurus slowly rose up on his huge hind legs and threw back his head. His sleep had been disturbed and he was angry. A little mammal, catching dragonflies in the ferns, had scampered over the sleeping giant's head. Now the tiny creature clung fast to a dead branch on the ground. His hair stood on end while the meat-eater searched him out.

Suddenly the breeze carried the bellows of duckbills up from the misty hollow, and Tyrannosaurus forgot his rage. He turned his head to listen to the dinosaurs, and the little mammal dropped to the ground and fled into the myrtle scrub.

Tyrannosaurus was hungry. The sound of the duckbilled dinosaurs made him feel even hungrier. He strode off in search of them. Every other creature fled as he moved through the thick undergrowth. Birds flew up before him and lizards darted out of his way.

As he marched the sky grew dark. Thunder rolled through the hills and rain poured from the black clouds. Branches bent and cracked under the force of the downpour. Tyrannosaurus pounded onwards, careless of the driving rain. But there was no chance of him catching the duckbills now. The thunder drowned their bellows and he was still too far away to pick up their scent.

By the time the storm had cleared, Tyrannosaurus was far beyond the woody hills. Ahead of him far across the plain he spied a herd of Triceratops. They were grazing on the warm, wet ferns that covered the sunlit ground. With no trees to hide him now, he had to move carefully. His prey must not know he was coming.

The hunter slowed his pace. Only the sound of his clawed feet rustling through the ferns could be heard. But that was enough. One Triceratops caught the sound and roared a warning to the rest. The animals bunched together in a tight mass of armor.

Only one animal was unable to reach the safety of the herd. She stood in the great reptile's path as he approached. She saw his sharp teeth flash in the sunlight and felt the ground shake as he began to thunder towards her.

At the last moment she wheeled and charged him. Her heavy body crashed into Tyrannosaurus and her sharp horn tore into his thigh. He bellowed with pain and limped away bleeding.

Tyrannosaurus was not only hungry now, but tired and hurt as well. He could not chase the Triceratops, so he rested for a while and then stirred himself again to look for food. He headed back to the valley. At the edge of the swampy river a clump of maidenhair trees grew. Feeding on these was a group of duckbills; and farther along the shore was a flock of pink wading birds.

The noise of the birds made it impossible for the duckbills to hear the dreadful tread of Tyrannosaurus. They went on eating. Then Tyrannosaurus charged, trailing blood from his aching thigh. The birds rose into the air like a pink cloud, their wings clattering. Without looking, one duckbill crashed into the water and swam for his life. The others followed it, struggling to reach the safety of the deeper water. Tyrannosaurus raged along the bank. He was too heavy to cross the swampy ground. There was no way for him to reach his prey.

For hours Tyrannosaurus prowled along the high ground by the edge of the river. A crocodile watched him from the opposite bank. Marsh turtles and terrapins plopped into the water as he passed. A pterosaur glided by and he lunged at it. But his great jaws snapped on empty air as the leathery wings brushed past him.

The sun dropped and a cool wind blew. The wind made the wound on the reptile's thigh sting with pain. Now he was too tired to hunt, so he limped to a clearing in a nearby redwood grove. There he stretched out on a soft bed of plants and went to sleep.

Tyrannosaurus slept peacefully. With nothing to fear from the sleeping giant, the other animals crept from their hiding places to hunt for food, or settled down themselves to sleep through the night.

Long after daybreak, Tyrannosaurus was still asleep. The morning chorus of birds was over and the plant-eating dinosaurs had long been munching the dew-sodden plants. They were well hidden by the giant green fronds of the ferns, so Tyrannosaurus did not see them when he woke. His leg was stiff and sore. It hurt when he walked, but he could not afford to rest any longer. He must find food.

He headed for the river again. On the way he heard a harsh scraping noise coming from behind some rocks. As quietly as he could, he looked over a crag and then let out a roar. Just below him was a Struthiomimus. The long-legged dinosaur was scraping the sand from a nest of new-laid eggs.

It had just smashed the shell of the first egg when Tyrannosaurus roared down on it. The dinosaur darted away, over the rocks into a dense grove of palms. Tyrannosaurus had no chance of catching the nimble creature. Once again his prey had escaped.

So Tyrannosaurus skirted the grove and continued towards the river. He could already smell the water when he saw before him the backs of a herd of alamosaurs. Their necks stretched high into the topmost branches of the trees. Some distance from the herd stood a young one, all on its own. It was busy eating fig leaves.

Tyrannosaurus raced forward. His great clawed hind foot slashed into the young dinosaur's body and his teeth sank into the back of its neck. The young Alamosaurus crashed to the ground, lashing its tail helplessly under the killer's weight. The other alamosaurs bolted away, as Tyrannosaurus ripped hungrily into his victim's flesh.

When Tyrannosaurus had gorged enough, he staggered away, bloated and drowsy. What remained of his victim's corpse was not left alone for long. The birds that had circled overhead while Tyrannosaurus ate his fill now swooped down to take their turn. And two scavenging dinosaurs darted in to seize a share of the feast. Tyrannosaurus walked back up the cliff. He was now no danger to any animal, though none was brave enough to approach him. He found a sandy hollow, sheltered by a tangle of magnolias. Here he lay down to sleep off his meal. The little reptiles and mammals that lived in the hollow kept well clear of the giant. When he woke he might be hungry again.

Facts about Dinosaurs

Ankylosaurus and Late Cretaceous North America

Length: 30 feet
Height: 9 feet

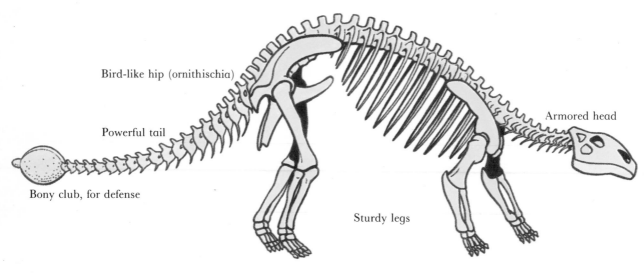

Bird-like hip (ornithischia)

Powerful tail

Bony club, for defense

Armored head

Sturdy legs

Skeleton of Ankylosaurus

When did Ankylosaurus live?

The Age of the Dinosaurs, or Mesozoic Era, began about 225 million years ago and lasted for some 160 million years. This immense length of time has been divided by scientists into three periods: the Triassic, the Jurassic and the Cretaceous. Ankylosaurus lived at the end of the third period, about 65 million years ago. It was one of the very last dinosaurs.

Where did Ankylosaurus live?

The fossils of Ankylosaurus have been found in the western part of North America, in the state of Montana and the province of Alberta. Today, this area of land is at the edge of the mighty Rocky Mountains which tower thousands of feet into the sky. When Ankylosaurus was alive, these mountains did not exist. In fact, the North American continent did not exist as we know it today. The earth movements that resulted in the formation of the Rockies, were, however, just beginning. The earthquake that flung Ankylosaurus down the slope in our story was a part of these earth movements. Across the millions of years, thousands of such earthquakes have pushed the rocks upwards to form the jagged peaks of today.

Today, to the east of the land where Ankylosaurus lived, are the Great Plains. 65 million years ago these did not exist either. A shallow sea stretched from the north of Canada through to the Gulf of Mexico. The world was a very different place when Ankylosaurus was alive.

The life of Ankylosaurus

Ankylosaurus belonged to one of the last and strangest groups of dinosaurs, the ankylosaurs. They first appeared during the early Cretaceous period, some 120 million years ago and lived a puzzling life. Ankylosaurus was around 30 feet long and weighed several tons, yet it had no teeth at all. Instead its jaws were covered in a horny beak. Scientists think that it probably ate soft plants and young shoots. Ankylosaur fossils are very rare. It is thought that this is because Ankylosaurus lived in the hills. The remains of animals that lived on high ground did not become fossilized easily. This may well explain the lack of Ankylosaurus fossils.

On its back the mighty Ankylosaurus carried a great weight of bony armor. Its tail ended in a heavy bone club that could have dealt a nasty blow to any attacker. Had a meat-eating dinosaur tried to attack Ankylosaurus, the plant-eater would probably have crouched down and swung its clubbed tail. It would have been impossible for any meat-eater to break through the armor and very difficult for it to overturn such prey. Even such a mighty hunter as Tyrannosaurus Rex would have found Ankylosaurus a very difficult animal to tackle.

Plants of the Cretaceous

At the time when Ankylosaurus lived, plants had been growing on dry land for nearly 300 million years, but in all that time there had not been a single flower. All the plants had been spore producers (gymnosperms). There were ferns and horsetails and though there were conifers, there were no true flowering plants. In the mid-Cretaceous period all that was to change. For the first time in the history of the earth the plant life would have been recognizable to us today. There were many trees that we know well: oaks, willows, maples and even the fig tree. Among the smaller plants of the time were wild roses, grape vines and heather. Ankylosaurus must have encountered plants very similar to those of our time. It has been suggested that the toothless Ankylosaurus ate the soft fruits of the new flowering plants.

Cretaceous animals

It was not only the plants of the days of Ankylosaurus that would have been familiar to us. Many of the animals would have been, too. Insects had been around for many years and had become as familiar as the dragonflies and beetles on pages 18-19. Mammals had also been walking the earth for a long time. However, the most advanced mammal alive at the same time as Ankylosaurus was the small shrew-like creature that Stenonychosaurus has caught on page 13. Mammals such as lions, gazelle and elephants did not evolve for millions of years. Birds had first evolved during the Jurassic period, almost a hundred million years before Ankylosaurus. By the late Cretaceous they had evolved into several different types.

Of course, many animals alive during the Cretaceous were very different from today's creatures. The pterosaurs that flew in the air are now long extinct. The dinosaurs that were then so common have also died out and look very strange to our eyes.

Palaeoscincus, a relative of Ankylosaurus, had spikes to protect the sides of its body, but no bony club.

Brachiosaurus and Late Jurassic Colorado

The Jurassic Period

The fossilized bones of Brachiosaurus have been found in rocks which are very old indeed. Scientists have managed to date these ancient rocks using a series of eras and periods. The Mesozoic Era, which means the era of middle life, began about 225 million years ago and ended about 65 million years ago. Scientists have divided this immense period of time into three periods. The first period is called the Triassic and lasted about 35 million years. The second period began 190 million years ago and ended about 130 million years ago. It is called the Jurassic period. The third period is known as the Cretaceous. The bones of Brachiosaurus have been found in rocks formed at the end of the Jurassic period. The dinosaur, therefore, lived about 140 million years ago.

The "Arm-Lizard"

Brachiosaurus means "arm-lizard" and scientists gave this dinosaur its name because of its peculiar bone structure. Its front legs were much longer than its hind legs, an unusual feature in the dinosaur world. Brachiosaurus belonged to the group of dinosaurs known as sauropods, one of the largest and most successful groups of the Age of Dinosaurs. Sauropods shared many characteristics in common. They were all plant eaters. They were all very large, and possibly grew up to 90 feet long. They all had long necks and tails. Most sauropods had hind legs that were longer than their front legs. Only Brachiosaurus and a few related species had longer forelegs. The reason for this has never been properly explained.

In the time when Brachiosaurus lived, the sauropods were the most important type of plant eater. There were more of them and they were larger than any other type of dinosaur. The lifestyle of the sauropods, however, has long been a source of disagreement among scientists. Even today, not all scientists agree as to how Brachiosaurus and other sauropods lived. This is due to the apparent inconsistencies of the skeleton. These creatures grew to an enormous size. It appeared that they could only support their weight by wallowing in water, much as hippopotami do today. Even if they walked on land, as is now believed, they could hardly have managed to move faster than a walk. Such slowness, combined with their lack of any weapons, left them wide open to attack by meat eaters. Under such conditions, their survival and success is puzzling. The tiny size of their mouths, compared with the size of their bodies, is another intriguing problem. It seems almost impossible that sauropods could eat enough to keep their vast bodies going, a situation which different scientists have used to try to prove a range of theories.

Skeleton of Brachiosaurus

Length: up to 90 feet
Height: up to 40 feet

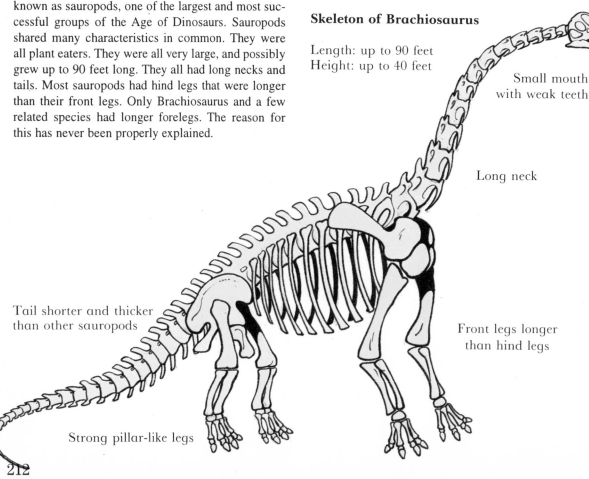

Small mouth with weak teeth

Long neck

Tail shorter and thicker than other sauropods

Front legs longer than hind legs

Strong pillar-like legs

Ornithopods later replaced
the sauropods as plant eaters

Iguanodon

Parasaurolophus

All in all, Brachiosaurus and its sauropod cousins are something of a puzzle. It can be stated that Brachiosaurus was one of the most massive animals ever to live on earth. In Morocco, Africa, scientists have found fossilized footprints of a dinosaur which would appear to have been 160 feet long. If so it would have been the largest animal ever.

Soon after this period, sauropods became increasingly rare as other dinosaurs took over their plant-eating role.

The environment
In late Jurassic times Colorado was a very different place from the plain and mountain state which it is today. The Rocky Mountains had not yet formed and even the Great Plains were a thing of the future. The climate too was very different. Throughout the world, warm wet conditions predominated and the humid day of the story was not at all unusual. Some plants of the time would still be familiar today: redwoods, monkey puzzle trees and conifers were the most common trees. Ferns and horsetails carpeted the ground. Others, such as the cycads and tree ferns, would appear strange. Perhaps the most noticeable aspect of the Jurassic flora, however, is the absence of some types of plants. There were no flowering plants at all and no grass grew anywhere.

The animal life of the time was far removed from that of today. Mammals now dominate the land, but in late Jurassic times they were unimportant, rat-sized creatures. Birds, now common, were then clumsy fliers. It was the dinosaurs which ruled the world. The most important plant eaters were the sauropods such as Brachiosaurus, Diplodocus and the smaller Haplocanthosaurus. Other plant eaters included the small Dryosaurus, Nanosaurus and Othnielia, which belonged to the Hypsilophodont family. Hypsilophodonts may have been small, but they were very successful and managed to survive for more than a hundred million years after the time of our story. Camptosaurus, which can be seen in our story wallowing in the mud with Brachiosaurus, was the earliest of the large Ornithopods. Over the millions of years which followed, the various types of Ornithopod would gradually take over from the sauropods as the dominant plant eating dinosaurs. The line of the Stegosaurus, perhaps one of the most famous dinosaurs, would soon die out completely.

There were two distinct types of meat eater in the late Jurassic. The small agile hunters were represented by Coelurus, which caught smaller animals. The larger hunters included Allosaurus and Ceratosaurus. These probably hunted the larger dinosaurs, though some scientists see them simply as large scavengers.

Dilophosaurus and Early Jurassic Arizona

The Day of the Dilophosaurus

The history of the world is very long and very complicated. Scientists only know about much of it by digging in the rocks and finding fossils. By looking at the rocks in which fossils occur, scientists can tell how old the fossil is. To help them do this scientists have divided the entire history of the world into eras and each era is further divided into periods. The dinosaurs lived during the Mesozoic Era which began about 225 million years ago and ended about 65 million years ago. The Mesozoic Era has been divided into three periods: the Triassic, the Jurassic and the Cretaceous. The fossils of Dilophosaurus have been found in rocks dating from the early part of the Jurassic period. This means that Dilophosaurus lived about 190 million years ago.

Arizona of long ago

The very first Dilophosaurus fossil to be discovered was found by a Navajo Indian in Arizona in 1954. From these remains scientists have been able to reconstruct the appearance and way of life of the dinosaur. Other fossils that have been found dating from the same time as Dilopho-

saurus have shown us the kind of world in which it lived. We know for instance that the area now known as Arizona was very different from the near-desert landscape to be seen today. The vegetation was rich and varied, and it was this which allowed the wide variety of animals to survive. Some of the plants would appear familiar to us today. There were conifers and monkey puzzle trees, as well as dozens of different types of ferns. Other plants, however, such as the cycadeoids and tree ferns have long been extinct and appear strange to our eyes. At the time, North and South America were not connected. They separated from each other a few million years before our story takes place.

Lifestyle of Dilophosaurus

Dilophosaurus was a large meat-eating dinosaur. It was about twenty feet long, which made it one of the largest animals alive at that time. Its powerful build and sharp teeth were ideal equipment for attacking other animals

Megalosaurus, a much larger relative of Dilophosaurus which lived in Europe.

Jurassic plants which are now extinct

tree fern

cycadeoid

and for eating meat. It belonged to a family of dinosaurs known today as the Megalosaurids, which means "great lizards". Megalosaurids were one of the most successful groups of dinosaurs. They lived over a period of many millions of years and evolved into numerous species. Dilophosaurus was different from other Megalosaurids because of the pair of bony crests on its head. These crests have puzzled scientists ever since the Navajo Indian first found fossils of this dinosaur. They are paper thin in places and would have been far too thin and fragile to stand up to rough treatment. It is possible that only males had these crests and that they were used as a type of display. In our story, Dilophosaurus uses them in this way when he tries to frighten the other Dilophosaurs away from his food.

Animals of the time

The animal life of the Early Jurassic was just settling down after a period of immense change. The dinosaurs had evolved a few million years earlier and had pushed most other forms of land reptiles into extinction. Segisaurus was an early member of the dinosaur family known as

Coelurosaurs. These small nimble hunters survived until the end of the Mesozoic. Ammosaurus was one of the last prosauropod dinosaurs. These creatures died out to give way to the Sauropods which were beginning to appear. Scutellosaurus was the last dinosaur to be found in early Jurassic Arizona. It was one of the earliest members of the Ornithischians, a large group of dinosaurs which became very successful millions of years after Dilophosaurus died out.

There were many other animals alive at the time, apart from dinosaurs. Many species of insect flew through the air, as did rather primitive Pterosaurs, the flying reptiles. Mammals could be found scurrying around in the undergrowth. One of these small mammals can be seen as a prey of Segisaurus in our story. Mammals remained small throughout the Mesozoic but later became the dominant form of land life and gave rise to man. In the sea lived several types of reptiles including the Plesiosaur which Dilophosaurus kills in the story and some species of Ichthyosaur. Ichthyosaurs were reptiles which looked like modern dolphins and were very successful.

Dimetrodon and Permian North America

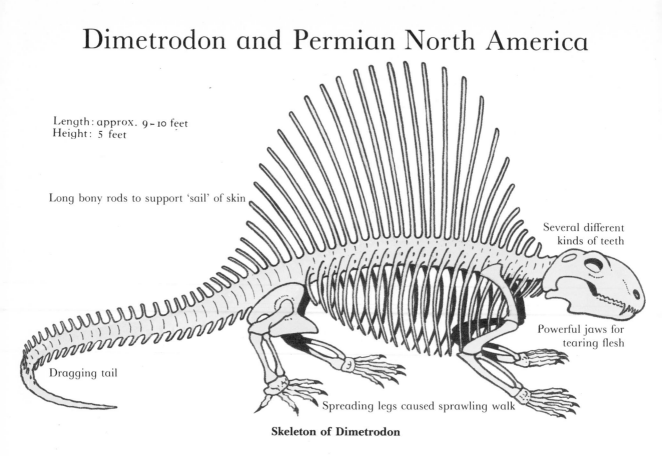

Length: approx. 9 – 10 feet
Height: 5 feet

Long bony rods to support 'sail' of skin

Several different kinds of teeth

Powerful jaws for tearing flesh

Dragging tail

Spreading legs caused sprawling walk

Skeleton of Dimetrodon

When did Dimetrodon live?

Life has existed on the planet Earth for hundreds of millions of years, perhaps even three and a half thousand million years. Scientists have divided this immense period of time into four main sections. The earliest were the Azoic and Proterozoic. These lasted from the earliest times until 600 million years ago and there was little life at this time. The second era is known as the Paleozoic, which means 'ancient life'. This era saw the rise of animal and plant life, most of which was in water. The third era began about 225 million years ago and is called the Mesozoic, or 'middle life' when living things managed to colonize the land very successfully and is marked by the ascendency of mammals and birds. The fourth era, our own, is called Cenozoic, 'recent life'. It began about 65 million years ago. Dimetrodon lived about 260 million years ago. This means that it lived at the end of the Paleozoic era. Scientists have divided each era into a number of periods based on changing life forms. The final period of the Paleozoic era was the Permian. It was during this period that Dimetrodon lived and hunted.

Where did Dimetrodon live?

The fossils of Dimetrodon and the other animals Dimetrodon encounters in the story were all found in Texas. However, in the far distant days of the Permian period, Texas was not a hot dry state at all. As can be seen in the story it was the site of a large, marshy delta. This was the mouth of a large river which flowed into a small sea whose shores ran along the Texas-New Mexico border.

The life of a Dimetrodon

Dimetrodon was a large, meat-eating reptile which measured some ten feet from nose to tail. In common with all other reptiles it was cold-blooded. This could have been a great problem. No animal can be very active unless it is warm first and cold-blooded animals rely on the heat of the sun or air to warm them up. During the night, reptiles lose most of their heat. A reptile as large as Dimetrodon would have taken nearly three hours to warm up. This was the reason for the large 'sail' on Dimetrodon's back. By turning the sail to face the sun Dimetrodon was able to warm up much more quickly, perhaps in less than an hour. This helped Dimetrodon to spend a lot more time hunting. On the other hand, a reptile cannot remain active if it is too hot. By turning its 'sail' into a wind or by sitting in the shade Dimetrodon could cool down and remain active better than other reptiles. This was why Dimetrodon was able to catch Diadectes. The smaller reptile was still sluggish because it had not cooled down after the mid-day heat. Edaphosaurus would have used its sail in a similar way.

Permian amphibians and reptiles

The Permian period was a time when amphibians and reptiles were both important groups of land animals. The reptiles, such as Dimetrodon, were relatively new but the amphibians had been around for almost a hundred million years and were highly successful.

The amphibians of Permian Texas included Cacops, Cardiocephalus, Ophiderpeton, Seymouria, Eryops and Diplocaulus. Of these the six foot long Eryops was by far the largest. It was one of the biggest amphibians ever. Nearly all of these Permian amphibians were doomed to extinction. Only Cardiocephalus, or a close relative, survived and evolved into today's salamanders, frogs and toads.

Diadectes may also have been an amphibian.

The amphibians were driven into extinction by changing earth conditions and were replaced by the reptiles which were to rule the earth for the next 200 million years. Reptiles of the time included Dimetrodon, Edaphosaurus, Petrolacosaurus and, perhaps, Diadectes. Dimetrodon and Edaphosaurus survived for many years, but then died out. A related group of reptiles, the therapsids, followed these two giants and eventually evolved into the mammals. The small,

and insignificant, Petrolacosaurus managed to survive and evolve. Some sixty million years later the descendants of this reptile evolved into crocodiles, dinosaurs and, later still, into birds. It is easy to understand, therefore, that Petrolacosaurus was a very important reptile.

Why the reptiles took over

We have seen that during the early Permian, when Dimetrodon lived, there were as many, if not more, amphibians than reptiles. By the close of the period, the reptiles were far more important and the amphibians became very rare indeed. How did this happen?

Perhaps the answer lies with the egg. Amphibians lay small, soft eggs in water. It follows that young amphibians hatch when they are under-developed and have to spend the first part of their lives in the water. The eggs of the reptile are different.

As can be seen in the illustration below, the egg of a reptile has a tough shell and a yolk, or food store. The reptile egg with its hard, protective shell can be laid on land. This means that the young do not have to go through a water-living stage. Instead they emerge as miniature adults, ready and eager to start eating at once. It was probably this advantage and the fact that the dry land, well away from water, was available to them as living space that finally ensured the reptiles an important place in the world.

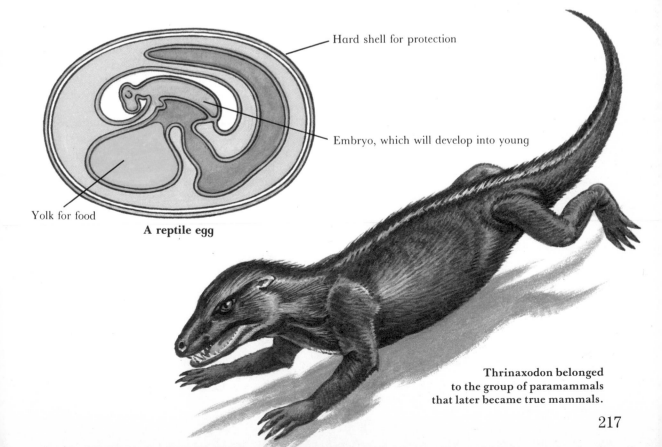

Hard shell for protection

Embryo, which will develop into young

Yolk for food

A reptile egg

Thrinaxodon belonged to the group of paramammals that later became true mammals.

Interesting facts about . . .
Diplodocus

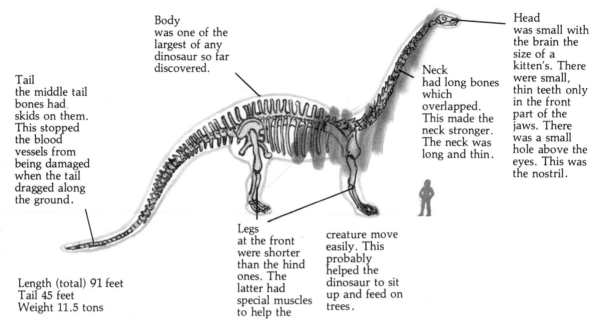

Body was one of the largest of any dinosaur so far discovered.

Head was small with the brain the size of a kitten's. There were small, thin teeth only in the front part of the jaws. There was a small hole above the eyes. This was the nostril.

Neck had long bones which overlapped. This made the neck stronger. The neck was long and thin.

Tail the middle tail bones had skids on them. This stopped the blood vessels from being damaged when the tail dragged along the ground.

Legs at the front were shorter than the hind ones. The latter had special muscles to help the creature move easily. This probably helped the dinosaur to sit up and feed on trees.

Length (total) 91 feet
Tail 45 feet
Weight 11.5 tons

The skeleton of Diplodocus compared in size to a human

Double beam
Diplodocus means "double beam". It belongs to a group of dinosaurs called Sauropods. These were the longest land animals ever to live on the earth. The only animal which ever grew any bigger was the blue whale.

Diplodocus had a very small head at the end of a long neck. This neck was about 26 feet in length. At the other end of the body was a whip-like tail, which was about 45 feet 6 inches long. Altogether the creature was about 91 feet in length. It probably weighed between 10 and 15 tons. As we said, Diplodocus was the longest creature ever to walk the earth. However, it wasn't the heaviest. Brontosaurus (which is known as Apatosaurus) weighed as much as 30 tons. This is five times the weight of a modern elephant.

Diplodocus had light bones
The backbone of Diplodocus was very light. Their bones were hollowed out. In spite of this it was still a very heavy creature. Its leg bones were solid to support its heavy weight.

Where did Diplodocus live?
At one time scientists thought that Diplodocus must have lived in water. Nowadays people have changed their minds. They think the creature lived in the swampy areas. They probably used their long necks to take leaves from high up on trees.

Why did scientists think Diplodocus lived in water?
Scientists believed the dinosaur lived in water because the creature had such small legs. These would not have held them up on land. Water is more buoyant and would support the creature more easily. When scientists first looked at the teeth of the Sauropods, including Diplodocus, they thought they were weak. This suggested to them that they could only deal with very soft plants like seaweeds. Soft plants grew in water.

Further studies on the teeth showed that they were not weak as they first thought. Evidently, Diplodocus ate hard plants. This was what caused their teeth to wear down.

Comparing Diplodocus to other water animals
Scientists have compared Diplodocus to other water animals. They have found that the shapes of the bodies of Sauropods are different. Most water animals have bullet-shaped bodies which help them move through the water more easily. They also have short necks. The feet of Diplodocus wouldn't have been much use in muddy conditions. They didn't spread out far enough. The creature would have gotten stuck in the mud.

Why Diplodocus was probably a land animal

All these are good reasons for thinking that Diplodocus was a land animal. However, there is one other reason. The weight of water pressing on the dinosaur's chest and lungs would have stopped it from breathing properly.

Dinosaur eggs

The Sauropods were egg-laying creatures like the other dinosaurs. Perhaps you would expect a creature as large as Diplodocus to lay a large egg. Actually, the female laid quite a small one. Many dinosaur eggs have been found. They were roundish in shape and probably about 10 inches in length.

When did Diplodocus live?

Diplodocus roamed the earth about 150 million years ago. This was during the Jurassic period. The age of Dinosaurs went from the Triassic (225 million years ago) to the Cretaceous (65 million years ago). The Jurassic was the middle one of these three periods.

Enemies of Diplodocus

There were many plant-eating dinosaurs which lived at the same time as Diplodocus. These included Brachiosaurus and Brontosaurus. There were also large, ferocious flesh-eating dinosaurs. These included Allosaurus, which was the largest. An agile Diplodocus would probably not have been attacked by Allosaurus. In fact, the young and old probably were.

Comparison of size between three Sauropods. Diplodocus was one of the longest Sauropods, although it was very light. Apatosaurus (Brontosaurus) was not as long as Diplodocus, but it weighed three times as much. Brachiosaurus was slightly longer than Diplodocus.

Brachiosaurus

Apatosaurus (Brontosaurus)

Diplodocus

Plesiosaurus and the Late Jurassic Oceans

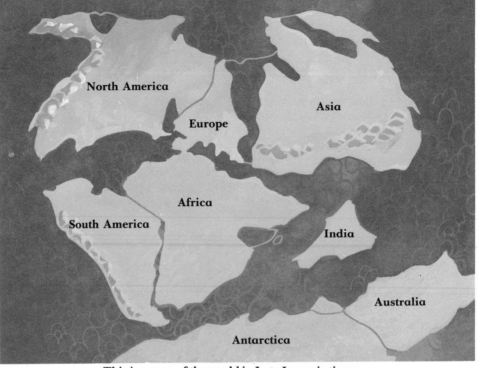

**This is a map of the world in Late Jurassic times.
The continents were in quite different places, as you can see. The Plesiosaurus
in the book lived in the sea to the left, or west, of Europe.**

When did Plesiosaurus live?

Plesiosaurus lived during the Age of the Dinosaurs. Known to scientists as the Mesozoic Era, the Age of the Dinosaurs began about 225 million years ago and ended about 65 million years ago. This immense stretch of time has been divided into three periods – the Triassic, the Jurassic and the Cretaceous. Plesiosaurus lived toward the end of the Jurassic, approximately 150 million years ago. Different types of plesiosaurs lived right up to the end of the Age of Dinosaurs.

Where did Plesiosaurus live?

Fossils of different types of plesiosaurs have been found in many parts of the world. It would seem that the plesiosaurs were a very successful group of animals which lived in all the seas of the world at the same time. The plesiosaurs in the book lived in shallow seas off the coasts of western Europe. All the animals in the book also lived in the same seas at the same time. Plesiosaurs living in other seas at other times would have encountered different animals in their lives.

The Discovery of Plesiosaurus

For millions of years the fossilized bones of the plesiosaurs lay below the sea floor. Later the rocks in which they lay were forced up by the titanic earth movements and became dry land. People then sometimes discovered the fossils but not until a mere hundred years ago did scientists learn about the giant reptiles of the Mesozoic.

Plesiosaurus may have been the very first giant reptile whose bones were found and studied. Hundreds of years ago, long before scientists had found out about dinosaurs and other giant reptiles, some strange bones were found in Germany. At that time, people thought that the bones belonged to winged dragons with long necks. The people who found the bones drew pictures of what they thought the dragons had looked like. If the wings in these drawings are replaced with flippers, the 'dragons' look very much like plesiosaurs. Scientists now think that the 'dragon bones' were really fossilized plesiosaur skeletons. In recent times plesiosaur skeletons have been found in the same part of Germany. One of the first complete plesiosaur skeletons to be discovered, was found more than a hundred years ago in England by a young girl called Mary Anning. Plesiosaurs have, therefore, been known to science for quite a long time.

The evolution of the Plesiosaurs

Though plesiosaurs lived during the Mesozoic Era, the Age of the Dinosaurs, they were not actually dinosaurs. The ancestors of the plesiosaurs belonged to a group which had produced the ten-foot-long Nothosaurus, some sixty million years earlier. Nothosaurus, and its relatives, were the most important type of reptile in the seas of the Triassic period. They had strong legs, unlike the flippers of Plesiosaurus, and spent much of their time on the land. It would seem that the nothosaurs were halfway along the evolutionary trail from a land reptile to a sea reptile, such as Plesiosaurus. By studying the fossilized skeletons of nothosaurs and plesiosaurs, scientists can discover many things. One of these is that the two groups belonged to a single, larger group. Indeed, it is possible that plesiosaurs were descended from nothosaurs.

At the beginning of the Jurassic period, about 190 million years ago, the line of the plesiosaurs split in two. Some plesiosaurs evolved long necks and small heads, others evolved short necks and long heads. Plesiosaurus, itself, was a member of the first group. The long-necked group culminated in the 45-foot-long Elasmosaurus which lived in the Cretaceous period.

If the long-necked plesiosaurs were large animals, their short-necked relatives became enormous. Pliosaurus, whose enormous head frightened the Plesiosaurus in our story, was a short-necked species. One kind, known as Kronosaurus, had a head twice as long as a man is tall, and measured fifty-five feet in length. Plesiosaurus was part of a very large family tree. Despite their numbers all the plesiosaurs and pliosaurs became extinct before the end of the Cretaceous period.

Other Reptiles of the Jurassic

Plesiosaurus was a very common type of reptile in the Jurassic seas, but there were many other kinds of reptiles alive at the same time. The land was dominated by three groups of dinosaurs. The most important plant-eaters were the enormous sauropods. Cetiosaurus and Pelorosaurus were both types of Sauropods and were both more than sixty feet long. The smaller hunters were Coelurosaurs, such as Teinurosaurus which can be seen making a meal of the baby Plesiosaurs on pages 116–117. The most powerful hunters of all were the carnosaurs. The thirty foot long Megalosaurus was a type of carnosaur.

Although reptiles first evolved on the land, many returned to the sea. Plesiosaurus was one of these. The ichthyosaurs were perhaps best adapted to life in the sea. These reptiles had evolved a body which was very fish-like in appearance and was ideally suited to a swimming life. Unlike plesiosaurs, the ichthyosaurs could not go ashore to lay their eggs and had to give birth at sea like whales and dolphins today. Metriorhynchus was a sea crocodile, literally a crocodile that took to a life at sea. Despite these adaptations the sea crocodiles died out within a few million years. At the time of our story, flying reptiles such as Rhamphorhynchus still ruled the air, although the first birds had already evolved.

Nothosaurus. Length: approx. 9–10 feet.

Elasmosaurus. Length: 45 feet

Protoceratops and Late Cretaceous Asia

Skull of Protoceratops

Beak for eating leaves of palm

Strong neck muscles to support head

Sharp teeth for slicing through the fibrous plants

Strong jaw muscles

When Protoceratops lived

Life in one form or another has existed on Earth for many hundreds of millions of years. Living beings have existed during the past 570 million years and scientists have divided this immense stretch of time into three eras. The earliest was the Paleozoic, the second was the Mesozoic, and the third, the Cenozoic. The Mesozoic is often known as the age of the dinosaurs and began 225 million years ago and ended 65 million years ago. It is divided into three periods: the Triassic, the Jurassic and the Cretaceous. Protoceratops lived near the end of the third period, the Cretaceous. This means it was alive about 75 million years ago.

Where Protoceratops lived

The fossils of Protoceratops have been found in rocks deep in the heart of the Gobi Desert. This great tract of barren land lies in Mongolia, in central Asia. Today the Gobi is cold and inhospitable but when Protoceratops roamed the region, the land was lush with plant life and animals. Many of the plants of the time would seem strangely familiar today. There were magnolias, conifers, ferns, oak trees and palms growing in profusion. The most important aspect of the plant life of the time was the appearance of flowering plants. Such plants had only been

on earth for a few million years when Protoceratops lived, but they were already the commonest plants and remain so to this day.

Lifestyle of Protoceratops

Protoceratops was a relatively small dinosaur. It was only about 6 feet long, but at the same time it was very heavily built. It therefore faced two problems of survival. Being small, it was easily hunted, and being heavy, it found running difficult. It managed to survive because of the bony armor of its head and perhaps by hiding in the forests. It certainly needed to stay close to palms for it would appear that these were its favorite food. Many Protoceratops' nests, similar to the one in the story, have been found by scientists. In common with other dinosaurs, Protoceratops probably looked after the nest and may even have cared for her young after they hatched.

Family tree of Protoceratops

Protoceratops was the earliest known member of a family of dinosaurs called Ceratopsians. All members of the family had the heavy build and bony head frill of the Protoceratops. Over the next few million years the Ceratopsians evolved into larger and larger forms and many sprouted huge, dangerous horns. The most famous of all

Ceratopsians is probably Triceratops. Triceratops was 30 feet long, weighed six tons and had three large horns. The Ceratopsian family continued to evolve and to become more numerous until they suddenly died out about 65 million years ago. At the same time all other dinosaurs died out, together with the pterosaurs and sea reptiles.

Animals of late Cretaceous Asia

The rocks of the Gobi Desert are rich in fossils and from these, scientists can tell which animals lived together with Protoceratops. Some of these animals appear in our story. Nemegtosaurus and Opisthocoelicaudia both belonged to a dinosaur family called Sauropod. These were the largest dinosaurs of all, but by the time of Protoceratops they were becoming much rarer than they had been. At the same time many new types of dinosaurs were appearing. Oviraptor is one of these dinosaurs. The family to which this egg stealer belonged did not appear until the time of Protoceratops. A slightly older family was that of the Dromaeosaurs, to which Velociraptor belonged. The family is distinguished by a large claw on the hind feet with which the animals were able to hunt ferociously. It was with good reason that Protoceratops was afraid of Velociraptor. The Nodosaur family first appeared at about the same time as the Dromaeosaurs. Nodosaurus itself was a huge beast some 18 feet long, but in time the family would produce even larger plant eaters. The largest meat eater of the time was the powerful Tarbosaurus. This huge beast was about 45 feet long and was probably the mightiest hunter of the period. Chingkankousaurus was much smaller than Tarbosaurus, but may have been more agile and therefore more dangerous to such animals as Protoceratops. However, it was not just dinosaurs which stalked the land so many millions of years ago. There were many other sorts of reptiles, including lizards, tortoises and snakes, together with amphibians and some mammals. Today mammals are the most important group of animals on earth. Man himself is a mammal and so are most of the large animals which live on land. During the times of Protoceratops, however, mammals were small and unimportant.

Two much later members of the Ceratopsian family

Triceratops

Styracosaurus

Interesting facts about . . .
Pteranodon

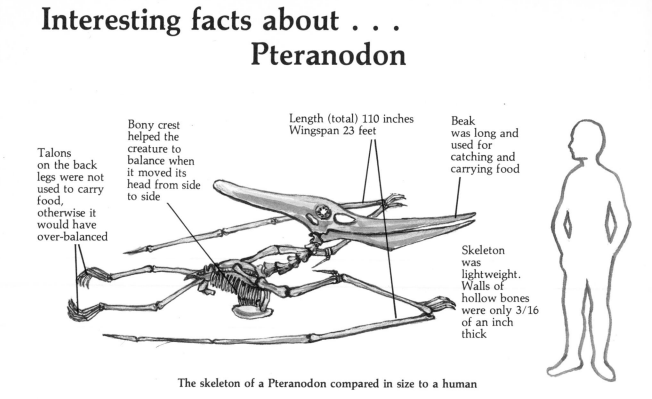

Talons on the back legs were not used to carry food, otherwise it would have over-balanced

Bony crest helped the creature to balance when it moved its head from side to side

Length (total) 110 inches
Wingspan 23 feet

Beak was long and used for catching and carrying food

Skeleton was lightweight. Walls of hollow bones were only 3/16 of an inch thick

The skeleton of a Pteranodon compared in size to a human

The Age of Dinosaurs

Although dinosaurs dominated the earth during the "Age of Dinosaurs", there were other creatures as well. Pterosaurs, which included Pteranodon and Pterodactylus, were among these. As the large dinosaurs roamed the land, large creatures were also flying overhead.

When did Pteranodon live?

Scientists divide the life of the earth into eras. Pteranodon lived during the Mesozoic Era which started 225 million years ago and ended about 65 million years ago. Each era is divided into periods. In the Mesozoic Era there were three periods. These are called Triassic, Jurassic and Cretaceous. The Triassic was the first and the Cretaceous the last. Pteranodon lived during the Cretaceous Period.

What was Pteranodon?

Pteranodon wasn't a dinosaur. It was a Pterosaur. Pterosaurs developed from reptiles. They were able to fly. If we look at Archosaurs like Podopteryx we can see similar features between these and Pterosaurs. Normally, when we think of reptiles we think of snakes and lizards. Pterosaurs

are different. They developed wings and could fly.

Pteranodon was one of the Pterodactyls. The oldest known Pterosaur is one called Eudimorphodon. This creature lived in Italy during the Triassic period. The smallest Pterosaur was Pterodactylus. It was about the size of a sparrow. Pteranodon was thought to be the largest Pterosaur. Recently, a bigger Pterosaur called Quetzalcoatlus was discovered in Texas.

What size was Pteranodon?

Pteranodon was a large creature. It had a wing span of about 23 feet. This is twice the wing span of the albatross which is the largest bird living today. From the place where the wing joined the body to its tip it measured 4 feet. The *total* wing span of an albatross is no more than 11 feet.

How did Pteranodon fly?

Scientists have been fascinated by Pteranodon. They have made models of the Pterosaur. They have tested these in wind tunnels. Pteranodon had leathery wings. The tests in the wind tunnels showed that it could fly well. When it flew over the oceans it used air currents. These often carried it a long way. Pteranodon would have spent much of its life gliding on these currents.

However, if it managed in the air, Pteranodon had problems on the ground. Tests showed that it would have found it difficult to take off from flat surfaces. Scientists are not sure what happened when the creature landed on the ground. When it had a place from which to launch itself, it could use the air currents to help it get into the air. There are many of these currents around cliffs and over the oceans. Birds living here today still use the same method. It means they don't have to use as much energy.

Scientists were puzzled by a strange crest which Pteranodon had on its head. At first it seemed that it added a lot of weight. This would make flying even more difficult. In fact, it only weighed about 6 oz. because it was made of thin bone. Tests showed that the crest helped Pteranodon to balance when it moved its neck. If the crest hadn't been there it would have needed large muscles. These would have made it even heavier.

What did Pteranodon feed on?

Pteranodon fed on fish. It had a long beak. It also had claws on its back legs. It didn't use these when fishing. If it had carried fish in these claws it would probably have overbalanced. The claws were used for hanging onto cliffs and ledges. When Pteranodon wanted to feed it could glide from the cliffs and pick up food. It could also land on water. When it was flying over the oceans it dived into the water to catch its food.

What were Pteranodon's bones like?

We have said that Pteranodon was large. Apart from its enormous wing span, its body measured 9 feet long. Scientists were surprised when they looked at the creature's bones. They were very thin. It was strange that the creatures managed to dive into the sea without breaking their bones. With light bones, Pteranodon found it easy to launch itself. It probably only weighed about 40 pounds, which was very light for its size.

Comparison of various "flying" creatures. Quetzalcoatlus was a pterosaur. It had a wing span of 33 feet compared with 23 feet for Pteranodon. Pterodactylus was less than 9 inches long.

Quetzalcoatlus

Pteranodon

Pterodactylus

Stegosaurus and the Jurassic World

Length (from nose to tail): 20 feet or more
Height (to top of plates): 16 feet
Weight: up to 1.8 tons

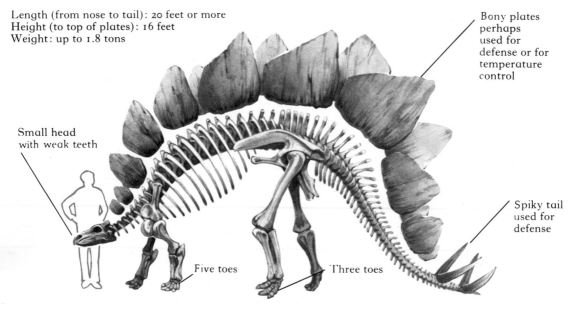

Bony plates
perhaps
used for
defense or for
temperature
control

Small head
with weak teeth

Spiky tail
used for
defense

Five toes

Three toes

The skeleton of Stegosaurus compared in size with a man

When Stegosaurus Lived

The Age of Dinosaurs is divided into three periods: the Triassic, Jurassic and Cretaceous. Stegosaurus lived during the Jurassic, about 150 million years ago.

What Stegosaurus Ate

We know from Stegosaurus's teeth that it was a plant-eater. (Meat-eaters have sharp tearing teeth, while plant-eaters have flatter teeth for grinding up tough leaves and stems.) Stegosaurus had a very small mouth with weak little teeth. So it must have spent a very great deal of its time feeding, in order to get enough nourishment for its great body. With such a short neck, too, Stegosaurus could have fed only on plants that grew low on the ground. These plants would have been mostly ferns and horsetails; there were almost no flowering plants during Jurassic times.

Enough for all

Stegosaurus did not have to share the low-growing plants with many other animals. Brontosaurus (see page 177) and the other tall plant-eating dinosaurs fed on tall plants, such as cycads (palm-like trees), maidenhair trees and conifers. Medium sized dinosaurs, such as Camptosaurus, fed on the lower branches of these trees. They stood on their hind legs to reach them. If you look at the animals that live today on the African plains, you will see the same thing. Giraffes, with their long necks, browse on the tree tops; gerenuks rear up on their hind legs to reach the lower branches; the other antelopes feed on the bushes and grass.

"Mini" Brain in a Monster Body

Stegosaurus must have been a very unintelligent animal. For, despite a huge body, it had a brain no bigger than a walnut. People once thought that Stegosaurus had two brains: there is a large swelling in its spine which seemed to be a brain. But this second "brain" was nothing like a real one. It was merely a mass of large nerves that Stegosaurus needed to control its huge back legs and tail.

A Deadly Weapon

With fierce meat-eaters roaming the land, plant-eaters needed sturdy weapons and armor to protect themselves. Stegosaurus's spiky tail was an excellent weapon. It could easily cripple a small meat-eater, such as Ornitholestes (see page 172). This "nuisance" probably hung around the stegosaurs waiting to snap up lizards and other small creatures stirred up by their huge feet. A blow from the tail could probably also have wounded a smallish meat-eater, such as Megalosaurus (see page 180), though bigger ones would not have been kept at bay for long.

Armor or Heating?

The double row of great bony plates along Stegosaurus's back looks very fierce indeed. Any attacker that attempted to strike Stegosaurus on the back would have had a dangerous and difficult time. But, since the plates did not protect the sides or legs at all, few animals would have been stupid enough to go for the back. What use then were the bony plates to Stegosaurus?

Some scientists think that the plates helped Stegosaurus to control its temperature. Such a large dinosaur would have got very hot as it moved about. When we get hot, we sweat, and sweating makes us cooler. But dinosaurs probably could not sweat. They would have had to find a cool place or go for a swim to get rid of the heat—unless they had some other way of cooling themselves. Stegosaurus's plates could have served this purpose. A large flat area cools down much quicker than a bulky body. A large flat area also warms up quicker. So if Stegosaurus was cold, it could turn its side to the sun. The heat striking the plates would soon heat the blood in them, and the warm blood would then flow all around the body, making the whole animal warm.

Early Death and Safer Successors

Being able to control its temperature (if it could) does not seem to have helped Stegosaurus to survive. The stegosaurs died out early in the Cretaceous period. The reason for their disappearance was probably that their weapons and armor simply did not give enough protection against the great meat-eaters.

During the Cretaceous a new kind of dinosaur took the place of the stegosaurs. The ankylosaurs (see below) were smaller but had far stronger armor. Like Stegosaurus, they fed on the low-growing plants, but they could escape injury by dropping on their stomachs.

Two types of ankylosaur

Scolosaurus

Ankylosaurus

Tyrannosaurus and the Cretaceous World

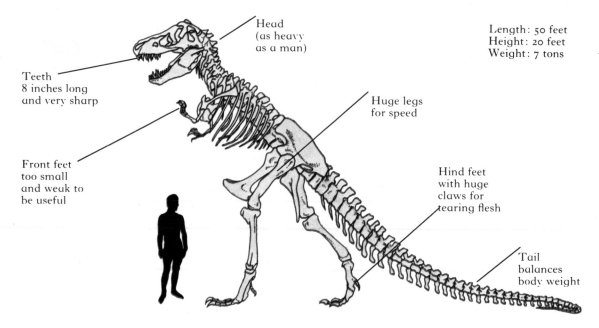

Head (as heavy as a man)

Teeth 8 inches long and very sharp

Front feet too small and weak to be useful

Huge legs for speed

Hind feet with huge claws for tearing flesh

Tail balances body weight

Length: 50 feet
Height: 20 feet
Weight: 7 tons

The skeleton of Tyrannosaurus compared in size with a man

The Age of Dinosaurs

The Mesozoic Era, or Age of Dinosaurs, was divided into three parts: the Triassic, Jurassic and Cretaceous periods. When Tyrannosaurus lived, about 90 million years ago, the Age of Dinosaurs was coming to an end and the world was changing.

During Jurassic times, the plants were mostly ferns, conifers and palm-like plants called cycads. In Cretaceous times there still were many conifers, but there were also flowering plants. Today there are more flowering plants —from daisies to big oak trees—than any other kind. But in Cretaceous times these plants were new. Two of the earliest kinds were magnolia and myrtle.

The Prehistoric King of Beasts

Tyrannosaurus was the largest flesh-eater ever to walk on earth and the master of his world. Running on his huge back legs, he leaned forwards and his great tail balanced the weight of his body. He brought down his prey with the sharp claws on his hind feet and killed it with his dagger-like teeth. His front legs would have been no help in a struggle. They were ridiculously small with only two clawed toes on each. Tyrannosaurus may have used them to steady himself as he rose from the ground, or he may have used them as tooth picks.

Attack and Defense

Tyrannosaurus was big enough and fierce enough to kill any animal. But first of all he had to catch his prey—and few animals allow themselves to be caught easily. Even the most peaceful have some form of defense, such as an ability to outrun or hide from the attacker, or weapons and armor to fight with. Most of them also live in herds which gives them more safety. A hunter is far more likely to attack an animal on its own than with others, and also there are more animals to give the alarm when danger threatens.

Like an elephant with a lion, the sheer size of Alamosaurus was enough to deter an attack. So Tyrannosaurus would not normally have tackled one unless it was so young or so old that it could not fight back (see page 207). An adult Triceratops (see page 196), weighing as much as eight tons, could also protect itself.

Perhaps the easiest prey for Tyrannosaurus were the duckbilled dinosaurs (hadrosaurs). These plant-eaters were a little smaller and much weaker than Tyrannosaurus. The strange "crests" on their heads looked like helmets or horns, but they were not in fact used for defense. The crests were connected to the nose: they may have helped the animals pick up an enemy's scent more quickly or made their bellows sound louder. Apart from that, the duckbills' only real chance was a swift dash, or the kind of lucky escape they had on page 198.

The plant-eaters did not only have the big meat-eaters to fight. There were many smaller ones. These could not kill them, but they could do them harm. Struthiomimus (see page 204) and the scavenging Ornitholestes (see page 208) would probably both have eaten the eggs of other dinosaurs and perhaps their young as well. The little mammals that lived in Mesozoic times may also have eaten dinosaurs' eggs.

In the Air

Nobody knows much about the birds that lived during Cretaceous times. Scientists think that they must have been much like the birds we know today. The wading birds on page 199, for example, were probably like modern flamingoes. The birds could fly well so they had few enemies to fear. The flying reptiles, the pterosaurs, could not really fly. They lived near seas or lakes and glided over the water, picking up fish and insects (see page 201).

The Death of the Dinosaurs

Tyrannosaurus and his giant relatives were among the last of the dinosaurs. At the end of the Cretaceous period, about 70 million years ago, they all died out. The Age of Dinosaurs was at an end. The little mammals grew bigger and bigger. Today mammals are the most important animals. What killed the dinosaurs? Nobody knows, for certain, but most scientists think that the world grew too cold for them. Only animals with fur or feathers (mammals and birds) could survive the cold.

Tyrannosaurus and some of his relatives. They all belonged to a group of flesh-eaters called carnosaurs

Tyrannosaurus   Allosaurus   Megalosaurus

Glossary

ALAMOSAURUS [AL-a-mo-SAW-rus] This long-necked herbivore fed on the tree tops. Its fossils were found in Texas, and it was named after the famous Alamo. *See pages 24, 206.*

ALLOSAURUS [AL-oh-SAW-rus] Its name means "different reptile." This carnivore grew to 40 feet in length and weighed up to 2 tons. It had a large head and blade-like fangs. This ferocious beast walked upright and hunted in packs. *See pages 38, 95, 213, 229.*

ANKYLOSAURUS [ANK-ee-lo-SAW-rus] Its name means "stiff reptile." This herbivore had tough, bony armor and a spiked tail for defense. It had to spend the whole day eating in order to satisfy its hunger. *See Chapter One; pages 210-211, 227.*

APATOSAURUS [a-PAT-oh-SAW-rus] Its name means "deceptive reptile." Another name for BRONTOSAURUS.

ARCHAEOPTERYX [AR-kee-OP-ter-ricks] Its name means "ancient wing." This narrow-beaked, winged reptile (Pterosaur) was the earliest known bird. It ate both insects and meat, and was about 12 inches long. *See pages 11, 175*

Dimetrodon

BRACHIOSAURUS [BRAK-ee-oh-SAW-rus] Its name means "arm lizard." This herbivore was the largest of all dinosaurs: up to 90 feet long, 40 feet high, weighing 100 tons. Its long neck enabled it to reach food in high tree tops. *See Chapter Two; pages 212-213, 219.*

Parasaurolophus

BRONTOSAURUS [BRON-toe-SAW-rus] Its name means "thunder lizard." Also known as APATOSAURUS. This herbivore had a small head and peg-like teeth. It weighed 30 tons, lived in herds on dry land, and ate about 1000 lbs. of food per day. *See pages 93, 176, 218-219.*

CACOPS [KAY-cops] This small amphibious dinosaur had bony plates on its back, and laid its eggs in water. *See page 75,217.*

CAMPTOSAURUS [KAMP-toe-SAW-rus] Its name means "bent reptile." This herbivore had a bird-like, horny beak. It was 16 feet long, weighed 1/2 ton, and could stand on its hind legs to reach for food, although it walked on all fours. *See page 35.*

Pterodactyl

CARDIOCEPHALUS [KARD-ee-oh-SEF-ah-lus] This tiny amphibian laid its eggs in water. Its modern-day descendants are the frog, the toad, and the salamander. *See page 75,217.*

CERATOSAURUS [ser-RAT-oh-SAW-rus] This ferocious carnivore was a fierce hunter. It grew to about 15-20 feet in length and had a peculiar horn on the top of its snout. *See pages 36, 213*

CETIOSAURUS [SEE-tee-oh-SAW-rus] Its name means "whale lizard." This herbivore weighed as much as three elephants, and measured 60 feet from head to tail. It had dull little teeth like most other plant-eaters. *See page 113.*

Rhamphorhyncus

CHASMOSAURUS [KAZ-moh-SAW-rus] Its name means "ravine reptile." This sharp-beaked herbivore had a small nasal horn and two big horns that jutted out from its brow. It had a short tail, button-like scales, and a large spiked collar. *See page 31.*

CHINGKANKOUSAURUS [chin-KANK-oh-SAW-rus] This carnivore was smaller and more agile than most of the larger hunters. This made it very dangerous, due to the speed of its fierce attacks. *See page 149.*

COELURUS [see-LOOR-us] Its name means "hollow tail." This carnivore was one of the earliest known dinosaurs. This scavenger was about 8 feet long, ran on its hind legs, and looked like an ostrich. *See page 32.*

Stegosaurus

DEINONYCHUS [dye-NONN-ee-kus] Its name means "terrible claw." This small carnivore was 9 feet long and 3 feet high. It had a long tail for balancing, could run very fast, and hunted in packs. *See page 11.*

DILOPHOSAURUS [dye-LO-fo-SAW-rus] This large and powerful carnivore was about 20 feet long, and had a pair of bony crests on its head. *See Chapter Three; pages 214-215.*

DIMETRODON [dye-MET-tro-don] Its name means "two-sized tooth." This carnivore measured 10 feet long, and had a "sail" on its back supported by spikes. It is believed that the sail may have worked like a radiator, helping the dinosaur to control its body temperature. *See Chapter Four;pages 216-217.*

Archaeopteryx

DIMORPHODON [dye-MORF-oh-don] Its name means "two-formed tooth." This winged carnivore had a blunt, short, heavy head armed with teeth, and a long bony tail and wings. *See page 30.*

DIPLODOCUS [DIP-lo-DOE-kus] Its name means "double beam." This leathery-skinned herbivore was the world's largest land animal, measuring 91 feet in length, with a whip-like tail measuring 45 feet. *See Chapter Five ;pages 49,218-219.*

DROMAEOSAURUS [DROM-ee-uh-SAW-rus] This small but fierce, bird-like carnivore was about the size of a grown human. A fast runner, it hunted in packs, and leaped on its prey with large, sickle-shaped claws. *See page 223.*

DRYOSAURUS [DRY-oh-SAW-rus] Its name means "wood reptile." This small herbivore was about 6-1/2 feet long. It was a fast runner, who fought by kicking with its small powerful legs. *See page 41.*

EDAPHOSAURUS[ee-DAF-oh-SAW-rus] This herbivore had a "sail" on its back, like the DIMETRODON, which helped to warm its body in the sun and cool it in the breezy shade. *See page 77, 217.*

ELASMOSAURUS [ee-LAZ-moe-SAW-rus] Its name means "plate reptile." This marine reptile had a long neck and a small head. It measured 45 feet in length and had 76 vertebrae in its flexible neck which was more than 1/2 the length of its entire body. *See page 221.*

Ornithomimus

ERYOPS [EAR-ee-ops] This fish-eater was roughly the same size as a seal. About 6 feet in length, this amphibian laid its eggs in the water. *See page 81,217.*

EUDIMORPHODON [you-dee-MOR-foe-don] This creature is the oldest known winged reptile or Pterosaur. *See page 224.*

EUOPLOCEPHALUS [you-OP-loe-KEFF-a-lus] Its name means "well-armored head." This heavily-armored herbivore weighed 4 or 5 tons, and was 20 feet long. Its tail ended in a large round club that was used as defensive weapon. *See page 161.*

Tyrannosaurus skull

HADROSAURUS [HAD-row-SAW-rus] Its name means "duck-billed lizard." This most successful of the herbivores had a duck-like, toothless beak. It had a crest on its head which was used to pick up an enemy's scent, and to make its bellowing sound louder. *See page 228.*

Triceratops

HYPSILOPHODON [HIP-sill-oh-foe-DON] Its name means "high-ridge teeth." This small, horny-beaked herbivore was one of the fastest creatures ever to live on Earth. It was 4-7 feet long, 2 feet tall, and it weighed 150 lbs. *See page 91.*

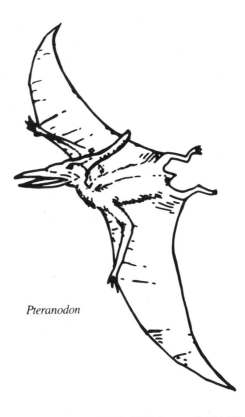

Pteranodon

ICHTHYOSAURUS [IK-thee-oh-SAW-rus] Its name means "fish-reptile." This air-breathing fish-eater resembled the dolphin and measured 33 feet long. It was a powerful swimmer and never left the water. *See pages 11, 122.*

IGUANODON [ee-GWON-oh-don] Its name means "iguana tooth." This two-footed herbivore had a "thumb" that acted like a bony spike. This spike was used as a defensive weapon, and sometimes grew to 10 inches in length. *See pages 10, 213.*

233

KRONOSAURUS [CROW-no-SAW-rus]
This large and powerful marine reptile
fed on other marine reptiles. It had
a very large head, measuring 10-12 feet
and an overall length of 55 feet.
See page 221.

LYSTROSAURUS [LIE-stro-SAW-rus]
This mammal-like herbivore lived a
semi-aquatic existence, similar to
today's hippo. *See page 30.*

Brontosaurus (Apatosaurus)

MAMENCHISAURUS [ma-MEN-
che-SAW-rus] Its name means "lizard
from Mamenchi." Named for the town in
China where its fossils were found, this
small-headed herbivore had the longest
neck of any dinosaur, reaching up to 36
feet in length. *See page 31.*

MEGALOSAURUS [MEG-a-low-SAW-
rus] Its name means "great reptile." This
large carnivore was one of the first dinosaurs to be discovered. It grew to 30 feet
in length. *See pages 119, 180, 214, 229.*

METRIORHYNCHUS [MET-tree-oh-
RINK-us] This fish-eating marine reptile
was a sea crocodile. Literally a croc that
took to a life in the sea. *See page 128.*

NANOSAURUS [NAN-oh-SAW-rus] Its
name means "very small lizard." This
herbivore was one of the smallest dinosaurs ever to live. *See page 41.*

NOTHOSAURUS [NO-tho-SAW-rus]
This marine reptile ranged from 1-1/2
feet to 20 feet in length, and had a back
fin and webbed feet. *See pages 11, 221.*

OPHIDERPETON [OH-fee-DERP-a-
ton] This snake-like amphibian laid its
eggs in the water. *See page 78,217.*

ORNITHOLESTES [or-nith-oh-LESS-
teez] This scavenging carnivore ate birds
and their eggs. It was very fast and nimble, and roughly 6 feet long. *See page 172.*

ORNITHOMIMUS [OR-nith-oh-ME-
mus] Its name means "bird imitator."
This toothless creature had a horny bill,
long, slender back legs, a long neck and
tail, and a small head. It was one of the
fastest of all dinosaurs. *See page 171.*

OTHNIELIA [OTH-nee-LEE-a] This
small dinosaur walked on its hind legs.
See page 44.

Iguanodons

234

PARASAUROLOPHUS [PAR-a-saw-ROW-low-fus] Its name means "rather like a ridged reptile." This duck-billed herbivore had an elaborate head crest which was used to enhance its sense of smell. *See pages 21, 213.*

PETROLACOSAURUS (PET-tro-LACK-oh-SAW-rus] After 60 million years on Earth, this dinosaur evolved into the crocodile. *See page 72.*

PLATEOSAURUS [PLAT-ee-oh-SAW-rus] Its name means "flat reptile." Some scientists believe that this herbivore was the first warm-blooded dinosaur. *See page 31.*

Triceratops

PLESIOSAURUS [PLEE-see-oh-SAW-rus] This fish-eating marine reptile laid its eggs on land. It propelled itself through the water with powerful, paddle-shaped limbs. *See Chapter Six; pages 11, 57 220-221.*

PLIOSAURUS [PLEE-oh-SAW-rus] This short-necked, large-headed, marine reptile was a powerful swimmer that set upon its prey in much the same way as the killer whale does today. *See pages 125, 221.*

Allosaurus

PROTOCERATOPS [PRO-toe-SERR-a-tops] Its name means "first horned face." This heavily-built herbivore was the first dinosaur to have a shield over its neck, and a horn on its head. *See Chapter Seven; pages 31, 222-223.*

PTERANODON [ter-ANN-oh-don] Its name means "winged and toothless." This leathery-winged, fish-eating Ptero-saur (*not* a dinosaur) rode the wind currents and carried food in its beak. *See Chapter Eight; pages 10, 224-225.*

PTERODACTYLUS [TER-oh-DACK-til-us] Its name means "finger wing." This was the smallest of the winged reptiles or Pterosaurs. It had a short tail, a horny beak, and long wing bones. *See pages 224-225.*

QUETZALCOATLUS (KWET-zal-CO-at-lus] Its name means "legendary or mythical bird." Its fossils were discovered in Texas in 1975. This largest of the winged reptiles or Pterosaurs had a wing span of over 33 feet. *See page 224.*

RHAMPHORHYNCHUS [RAM-foe-RINK-us] Its name means "beak snout." This carnivorous winged reptile, or Pterosaur, had broad wings, and resembled a crow with a long tail. *See pages 10, 116.*

SAURORNITHOLESTES [saw-RAW-nee-tho-LES-tes] This carnivore used the huge claw on its hind foot to kill its prey. *See page 28.*

SCOLOSAURUS [SKO-low-SAW-rus] This armored herbivore had massive bony spikes on its body and tail, which provided protection from predators. *See page 227.*

SEGISAURUS [SEE-ge-SAW-rus] This nimble carnivore was about the size of a rabbit. *See pages 53, 215.*

SEYMOURIA [see-MORE-ee-ya] This 24-inch long "missing link" between amphibians and reptiles was one of the first creatures to lay its eggs on dry land. *See page 81, 217.*

Tyrannosaurus

Plesiosaurus

STEGOSAURUS [STEG-oh-SAW-rus] Its name means "roof reptile." This platebacked herbivore had bony spikes that projected sideways from its tail. It was one of the first dinosaurs to become extinct. *See Chapter Nine; pages 49, 226-227.*

STENONYCHOSAURUS [ste-NON-ee-cho-SAW-rus] This carnivore's large eyes enabled it to hunt in the dim light of dawn, before its prey could fully see. *See page 12.*

STRUTHIOMIMUS [STROO-thee-oh-MY-mus] This toothless egg-stealer had long legs and was one of the fastest land animals ever to roam the earth. *See page 204.*

STYRACOSAURUS [sty-RACK-oh-SAW-rus] Its name means "spiny reptile." This large-headed herbivore had a long nasal horn and an elaborately frilled collar of spikes. *See page 223.*

TARBOSAURUS [TAR-bow-SAW-rus] This 45-foot long carnivore was a mighty hunter. *See page 146.*

TEINUROSAURUS [TIE-new-row-SAW-rus] This small carnivore was a fast runner and a dangerous hunter. *See page 117.*

Stegosaurus

Ichthyosaurus

THRINAXODON [thrin-AXE-oh-don] Its name means "trident tooth." This "paramammal" was later to develop into one of the first mammals on Earth. *See page 217.*

TRICERATOPS [try-SERR-a-tops] Its name means "three-horned face." This herbivore resembled a huge rhino. Its nasal horn was short, but a pair of 3-foot long horns projected from its brow. These horns were used for defense, not attack. *See pages 26,163,197,223.*

TYRANNOSAURUS REX [tie-RAN-oh-SAW-rus recks] Its name means "tyrant reptile." The largest carnivore ever to walk the earth, this 50-foot long. 20-foot high king of the meat-eaters weighed 7 tons. *See Chapter Ten; pages 228-229.*

VELOCIRAPTOR [VEE-low-sir-RAP-tor] This long-legged carnivore had huge claws on its hind feet, and hands that could grasp its prey. *See page 139.*